THE FINANCIAL FREEDOM GUARANTEE

possible without the excellent mentorship of my property investing guru Marco Robinson."

— **Azlan Adnan**

"Marco Robinson, you made my dream come true which in turn channelled and opened the gateway to help a lot of others. It was all by believing in me and paving the way to my future success."

— **Josie Wachi,** Alabama (of Josie Wachi Fashion Jeans)

"Marco Robinson, I had the pleasure of meeting him in KL in his office for about 45 minutes. The meeting was arranged by one of his sales licensee in Singapore. In that 45 minutes, the summary was, "Know what you want and go all the way…!" Today I am the vice president of Sales and Marketing at GToken VenVici.com. Thanks bro. Your words came at the right time when my vision about where I want to go was blurred! You are God blessed!"

— **Marcus Maximus**

"I saw where you were … I see where you are … phenomenal! You are driven by I don't know what? But you are something else, proud to know you. Respect!"

— **Michael Sweetmore**

"Marco. Inspiration and fearless game changer, showing everyone that you can and will be free. So honored to call you my friend."

— **Stuart Ockenden**

"Leader of Leaders … Marco Robinson has a complete understanding of creating your own reality! With so many people who "wish" they could be all they could be … Marco constantly leads by example in achieving anything he truly wants for himself by walking the talk. He has an amazing ability in being able to conceive it, believe it, and then follow through and achieve it. With an uncanny ability in his own way, pay it forward to show others how they too can create their own reality and be anything they want to, have a deep-rooted inner desire to, achieve. You just need to look at his life as a testament to this. I have always been proud to call Marco not only a colleague, more importantly a close personal friend, who continues to inspire all that choose to accept his advice and teachings with an incredible way of keeping it simple so that anyone can live the life they want to live, while most people only dream. If there were a tag line that I believe suits Marco it would be Nike's ... JUST DO IT! Thanks for the inspiration over the last twelve years of knowing you, even at times when you are not aware of it. I wish you all the success that you have created for yourself as your journey continues and for all those that are fortunate enough to cross your path that want the same for their lives."

— **Rob Salyer**

"I am Marco Robinson's mum and can say honestly say he was intensely focused and driven from young. I used to take him around England every weekend so he could compete in cycle races and could see even then that he would go on to great things. I feel privileged to be his mother and to have the great joy of still being part of his life and watching him grow even further whatever he does. He is the most generous and caring son any mother could wish for and he shares his ideas and good fortune with everyone. An awesome mentor and businessman. Proud mum."

— **Yvonne Poirier**

"Because you have a purpose, and I guess it has to be "creating wealth for everyone." Listening to you again and again is very inspiring for me! Thanks for all of the hard work you've done. May God bless you more. Your passion is contagious, it's endemic!"

— **Khairul Fahmi**

"Marco Robinson gave me the confidence and knowledge to move my business from the United States to countries all over the world. Previous to meeting him we just dabbled in the international markets. Over the past two years his partnership, knowledge, and amazing network of investors all over the world has helped us reach customers and partnerships we never would have been able to connect with previously."

— **Aaron Adams**

"I wish my school teacher was Marco Robinson when I was a kid back then, so that I could have become one of those young, self-made millionaire in the 90s. You are a great mentor to many, Mr Robinson. Thank you for sharing your priceless knowledge at a fraction of a cost."

— **Roger Choo** C K

"I've known Marco Robinson for almost ten years now... in that ten years, there's definitely been up and down for me, but one thing constant and consistent with Marco Robinson, he's a true entrepreneur with brilliant ideas, and the know-how to get there and help you get there. One thing about him that truly inspired me is his ability to manifest and give his best whether it's a good time or bad time for him. Whenever I need business advice, he's there, has never turned me down and he is a great mentor. A true entrepreneur, business mentor, with great vision and passion."

— **K.D. Ismalasari**

"Through his leadership course, Marco has been able to give our people astonishing breakthroughs in knowing themselves and improving their leadership and communication skills. The results speak one word, awesome! There was not a dry eye in all our sessions with Marco, as he managed to touch all our hearts in incredible ways. We have never experienced that kind of breakthrough in any other training we have undergone. Our communication and results have improved immeasurably, and I personally and my team cannot wait to have Marco back!"

— **Wesley Chuah**

About His People's Choice Award

"Absolutely fantastic, Marco. You deserve it."

— **Reza Maleki**

"So fantastic and much deserved. From humble beginnings to what you have achieved now. The fire, the spirit, generosity and the positivity is awesome and rubs off on everyone. Congratulations with much love."

— **Heidi Osfield Kean**

"I'm very happy to hear that. Marco Robinson, you deserve the award. I have learned a lot from your book and free workshop. Also from your Facebook, I read all the latest updates by you."

— **Jagdip Singh**

"Marco! Marco! Your energy is contagious! A man who is always there to help anyone who wants to succeed. You are a great inspiration! From the humble beginnings when you first came to our land ... to a man to be reckoned with. Kudos! Thank you for seeing and believing in my vision in workforce empowerment and nudging me! You hosted our launch and that was truly awesome and memorable. Thank you for believing in the impossible! Muuuah."

— **MiniWorkShopSeries.com**

"You gave me inspiration to leave my comfort zone, to think logically and go ahead with my dreams. Kudos for your great award nomination. Excellent timing!"

— **SPeed Perry**

"Marco Robinson, we have worked together for over three years now and from the very beginning your advice and strength hit me like a tornado. Your passion to do better and become whatever it is you dream to become is completely infectious and has helped countless people all over the world make their dreams come true. I am one of those people who have been inspired by your words and most importantly actions and I shall continue to develop, grow, and build my dream life thanks to your help, push, knowledge, and determination to just get out there and do it. You are a crazy monkey like me and I believe strongly that our energies were brought together to create and develop amazing things in our lives and to help and inspire others to do the same. We are now working together on many new projects and it is extremely exciting for me to be a part of your business and it is my honor to always do what I do for you. It is the least I can do to show you my appreciation for the help, guidance, and drive you have shared with me over the last few years. Congratulations on all your upcoming achievements, you do deserve it. Rock 'n roll."

— **Carl Graham**

About His First Book

"This is not just a book you're getting, Marco Robinson's valuable years of experience, techniques and most importantly his mindset of success! If you're looking for ways to achieve breakthroughs in selling, this is the man who understands salesmanship and communication more than anyone else I've ever met, PERIOD! Most books will just teach you the techniques of selling and leave you 'empty' at the end of reading ... but not so with this book. Not only will you uncover new strategies behind the concept of selling, you will also discover your hidden potential that will lead you to greater business and personal wealth."

— **Patric Chan**

"Whether you're a seasoned salesperson or you're taking your first tentative steps into the dynamic world of selling, when you read this book, know that you're in safe hands. There is something for everyone. When you follow the process Marco Robinson outlines, your results will skyrocket. Marco is a consummate professional, a person of extraordinary ability and someone who is totally passionate about other people's success. Read it and you will be well rewarded."

— **Paul Counsel**, Ph.D (http:www.paulcounsel.com.au)

"I've known Marco Robinson since 2002, when I met him at a seminar. I picked him as my buddy out of over 1,000 people. Why? To this day I'm not sure. I do know that my life has never been quite the same since. I've never met anyone who comes close to Marco when it comes to energy, personality, and persuasive power. In terms of his ability to influence, Marco is simply irresistible! I'm very proud to have been asked to recommend this book, which I believe is destined to take the place amongst the sales classics. I couldn't put it down! The only complaint I have is that he didn't write it sooner!"

— **Bob Scott**, Ph.D.

"I want to express my utmost gratitude to you. I've benefitted a lot from reading your book. With zero sales background, I've closed a deal on my first corporate appointment on the spot. The prospect was so excited and happy with my offer, they went to the ATM immediately and gave me $8,100 cash!"

— **Lai May Leng**

"Best book I have ever read. Transformed my results and would you believe it, I now managed to put a deposit down on a condo. Truly inspirational, very effective, practical, and awesome. Don't miss the workshop with the book, it will save your life."

— **Sherifah Alsagoff**

THE FINANCIAL
FREEDOM
GUARANTEE

THE 10-STEP AWARD WINNING PROPERTY BUYING SYSTEM
ANYONE CAN USE TO REPLACE THEIR SALARY, FIRE THEIR BOSS,
AND NEVER WORK AGAIN

MARCO ROBINSON

New York

THE FINANCIAL FREEDOM GUARANTEE
THE 10-STEP AWARD WINNING PROPERTY BUYING SYSTEM ANYONE CAN USE TO REPLACE THEIR SALARY, FIRE THEIR BOSS, AND NEVER WORK AGAIN

© 2017 **MARCO ROBINSON**.

Published in New York, New York, by Morgan James Publishing. Morgan James is a trademark of Morgan James, LLC. www.MorganJamesPublishing.com

The Morgan James Speakers Group can bring authors to your live event. For more information or to book an event visit The Morgan James Speakers Group at www.TheMorganJamesSpeakersGroup.com.

ISBN 978-1-63047-930-5 paperback
ISBN 978-1-63047-931-2 eBook
Library of Congress Control Number:
2015921346

In an effort to support local communities, raise awareness and funds, Morgan James Publishing donates a percentage of all book sales for the life of each book to Habitat for Humanity Peninsula and Greater Williamsburg.

Get involved today! Visit
www.MorganJamesBuilds.com

CONTENTS

INTRODUCTION

Would you like to fire your boss and never have to slave for a salary again?

You only live your life when you love your life. You find what you love to do with your heart, you figure out how to monetize it with your brain. And miracles will happen— miracles so mind blowing, you'll swear there was divine intervention.

If you're reading this book, it's because you want to be in control of your life rather than caught up in the rat race and an impossible job market, which will result in two things: unhappiness and never enough money to be independent and to do what you really love.

Well, guess what, 98 percent of the planet is in the same situation as you. They too are lost for answers, getting further into debt, and getting paid less and less as inflation and the years march on.

In this new book, for the first time, I am going to reveal my "Ten-Step Blueprint for Financial Freedom." This blueprint will allow you to replace your salary with *passive income* from assets you own, fire your boss, and finally live life on your terms.

You are likely thinking there is no way you can achieve this, and perhaps that the author is full of BS! This is the reaction I always get when I speak at my workshops. People want financial freedom but they don't believe they can make that happen. In this book you will learn that financial freedom is not only possible but that it's not really that difficult when you put your mind to it and follow the blueprint I have developed and mastered.

Consider me, basically a school dropout at 16 with no qualifications whatsoever, no certificates of training, absolutely nothing. I was shy, had a loser mindset, and held a lot of fear inside of me—so much so I couldn't string a sentence together without stuttering. At 34 (twelve years ago), I was able to fire my boss and replace my salary and then ...

I made myself into a multi-millionaire, became an award-winning entrepreneur, owning several businesses and over 200 properties throughout the world. (I will reveal actual case studies in this book).

I became a number-one, bestselling author, with my first book, *Close the Deal and Suddenly Grow Rich* (2009).

I became the owner of more than 300 hectares of agricultural land (800 acres), growing a commodity that has tripled in value in the past three years.

I took home the iProperty.com People's Choice Award for Best Real Estate Investment Company 2014–15, in Singapore. This was largely because of my prudent sourcing & purchase of thousands of remarkable properties that have given my students enough passive income and positive cash-flow to fire their boss for good. (Some of the actual case studies will be revealed in this book).

I was officially honored for work and contribution in Indonesia, receiving the title of Dato' Seri, S.T.M.P (equivalent to a knighthood in England). And there's more:

- I fulfilled a lifelong dream of starting a foundation called Female Entrepreneurs Made Easy (FEME).

- I started my own brand called NAKED, with a restaurant chain called NAKED: Experience the Passion, and won *Malaysia Tatler*'s Best Restaurant, 2015. This brand has spawned several franchise businesses, including NAKED Pizza, NAKED Coffee, and NAKED Beauty, a High Street beauty salon and makeup range.
- I became a leading actor in an adventure movie.
- I became a DJ, known as DJ Naked.
- I trained like crazy, achieved six-pack abs, and started modeling professionally at the age of 46.

I am not sharing these accolades to show off, I am sharing because I genuinely believe you can do even better than me and do it faster than I did. I truly believe whatever you want is entirely possible. It is only the way you think that prevents you from achieving the success you crave.

Because I reprogrammed my mindset and myself to generate residual income (money that comes in without having to work for it), I was able to create a life that I had always dreamed of.

I know you can do it because I have created a step-by-step blueprint that guarantees it. And it's not just any ol' guarantee, it's a guarantee I will stand by no matter what test you put to it or how you pick it apart. I am telling you right now this blueprint works so effectively that some of you in the next few weeks after applying it will be walking into your boss's office and telling him or her, "You're fired!"

How would you feel if you were able to set yourself free? Everyone I speak to is from a different background with a different set of circumstances. However, they all have one thing in common, they are not rich, and they are struggling to make ends meet every single day.

Why are there so many people like this? Simply, they have chosen to be an employee and operate with an employee's mindset. They have chosen, mostly unwittingly and unconsciously, to follow a system that is only equipped to produce employees and not fully empowered, financially free individuals who can change the world. The bottom line is: if you are not financially free it is your choice and you are responsible for it, but you might not know it yet, when you read this Book, you will!

I find myself in the most ironic situation when I give financial freedom workshops: the audience members often have credentials, qualifications, PhDs and master's degrees coming out of their ears, and yet they are broke and paid good money to listen to me—a high school dropout with no academic qualifications at all!

Isn't it crazy that people cannot get a degree or any conventional education to learn how to be financially free? Our present education system does not teach it yet the entire world wants to be financially free.

Instead, we put our children through the same 3,000-year-old education system (which, by the way, started in Greece) year after year and expect them to be successful and to be independent. But these kids end up borrowing money from their parents to survive. And they don't know any other way to make money than to work for people in jobs they often don't like.

Does anyone really love their job? In my own recent survey, 99 percent of people polled would rather give up working because they just don't love doing it.

When you are financially free, you have choice. You have a choice who you spend time with, what you're going to do, when to do it, and where to do it, without ever asking anyone's permission. You are in essence free to do what the hell you like and you're getting paid to do it.

Hands up, who would like to go to work on Monday morning and tell your boss, "You're fired! I have always hated this job, and you're horrible and you smell"? (They surely have some faults you've never had the courage to tell them.)

But people are afraid that if they leave their jobs, they will have no income to pay the rent and bills, and they will be poor for the rest of their lives. Well here's the truth, ladies and gentlemen: If you don't fire your boss, you will always be broke.

Why? Because your limited salary non-performs in many ways such as:

1. Most people don't get raises or if they do, not even enough to keep up with increases in costs of living.
2. Your salary is basically the sum of all the hours you work. This means that you are worth exactly your hourly rate and no more; meaning, if someone (or something—a robot or artificial intelligence—can do your job faster, more efficiently and more effectively for the same price, you will be replaced in a heartbeat! (Sadly, economics trumps sentiment all the time, especially in these very challenging economic times.) But this applies to employees, not the financially free).
3. Your job is not safe. The 2008 financial crisis was the worst economic time in the last eighty years. The last time things were that bad was the Great Depression of 1929. Apart from that, as mentioned in an article written by global strategist Adam Robinson (no relation) many factory-type jobs in today's economy will soon be taken over by robots and artificial intelligence.
4. If you get fired, you lose your source of income. Have you learned any other way to make money other than to get a job? Most likely not, which means the first thing you will do when you lose your job is look for another. Because that's how you have been programmed. And if you don't change your programming, you will always be looking for another job, which will guarantee that you will continue to be broke.

But don't just take my word for it. Let's take a look at some statistics. In America, with the largest welfare system in the world, out of every 100 people that retire at the age of 65:

- 1 is financially free,
- 4 are still working because they have to,
- 36 are dead and,
- 59 are dead broke, meaning they're in survival mode, living hand to mouth, paying debts back for the rest of their lives.

What about pensions and retirement funds, you ask? The average amount of money in 2008 in US 401(k) retirement plans was $129,000. A year later in 2009 that number dropped to $61,000! How would you feel if you lost more than half of your life's savings in a year?

If this happened in Iceland they would have jailed the people responsible (the bankers). In the United States and the rest of the world those same bankers are still operating with your money, because they have been given free rein by the government to operate without any regulation or rules of trading. I know it sounds hard to believe, scandalous in fact, but 98 percent of the world empowers the governments and the bankers to do what they want because they believe these are the people who know best. If that were the case:

Why does it seem like countries are going bankrupt every few months?

Clue: Your money is not spent correctly and goes into too many pockets rather than infrastructure. Then governments raise taxes and call it austerity measures.

Why are welfare systems out of control?

Clue: Because governments need votes to stay in power and need the unemployed to spend money to improve the economy.

Why are you always just surviving and never able to get ahead?

Clue: Because you have been programmed and conditioned to survive by your parents, your schoolteachers, your boss, and the people you hang around with. Later, I will get to why you are not making enough money and why you will continue not to make enough money if you don't change your thinking.

This book will show you how you can follow my blueprint and become financially free quicker than you ever imagined. And there has never been a better time to do so. There are more opportunities now to make lots of money than ever before. When you are able to see these opportunities, there is a very strong possibility you will be compelled to take action to follow the blueprint and start living your life for you instead of for somebody else!

Before I take you on this journey, understand the two irrefutable laws you must abide in order to be financially free, rich and successful. You cannot follow one and not the other or it simply will not work. These are:

1. In order to get what you want you will have to spend most of your time with people who have what you want.
2. You will have to remove yourself from the people who have what you don't want!

If I had to tell you the one thing that has made me very successful, I would have to say it is those two laws. Now, let's get on with it and get you started on your path to financial freedom.

THE FINANCIAL FREEDOM GUARANTEE
SNEAK PREVIEW

Let's get right to it. You see this property below?

Before 2008, this property cost more than $220,000. It has five bedrooms, three bathrooms, and 19,000 square feet of land, all freehold. It's fully renovated, with a new roof, new kitchen, new floors, new wiring, new bathroom—new everything. It's also in a beautiful suburb of an award-winning city, which is home to many Fortune 500 companies and has a growing population.

This property in 2012 cost me $65,000. I spent $20,000 renovating and attracted a great tenant within eight weeks. This property now generates these returns:

Net rental per month (after management fee, insurance and all costs including property tax)
= $1,150 (16.23% net yield annually)
Mortgage of $85,000 at 1.2% interest rate
= $300 per month
Net cashflow
= $850 per month!
Plus, a capital gain in the past six months
= 29.31% (more than $25,000 of equity and value added)

This deal was closed with absolutely no money down! That means I did not use any of my own money at all.

The question is why are you *not* doing this? Because you don't know how and you are programmed not to. Don't let fear of failure hold you back. I do this all the time, as this is part of my blueprint.

Here's what you really need to think about now! If your net salary is $2,000 per month after taxes, how many properties just like this would you have to buy in order to replace your salary? Answer: You would have to buy two and a half properties!

You would have to borrow $255,000, unless of course you have $255,000 floating around in your bank account. (Blueprint says: don't ever keep that amount of money in a bank account; you could lose it—yes, even when it's kept "safely" in a bank).

If you invested all that cash you would clear more than $3,000 net every single month. That's still a 16.23 percent return on your cash—cash on cash! If you instead deposited that cash in a savings account, your returns would range from 0.3 percent to (in a fixed deposit account) about 3 percent. So the choice is:

16% ($3,450 per month)

or

3% ($100 per month)

Which would you prefer? It shouldn't be a tough choice to make. You cannot live on $100 per month, so you would have to dip into your hard earned savings. Eventually you would spend all of it. How long is it going to take you to save $255,000 with your current salary? It might take forever and you would have to keep on working without freedom. But you can live on $3,450 a month *and* have an asset that is growing in value to protect your income.

Follow the blueprint and it will guide you to complete financial freedom. Without it, you will face virtual incarceration and slavery for the rest of your life!

You see, so called "financial advisers" (who, by the way, are not financially free) will make things so complicated, advising you to invest in some kind of managed fund that they will take care of for you because "you don't need the headache," they will say. But it's more to do with their earning a commission off of you than concern for your well-being.

Unwittingly, you will have caused, and be solely responsible for, the biggest headache of your life. You'll have just engineered your financial downfall in the space of ten minutes by signing a piece of paper that is supposed to guarantee your financial future.

WHY PROPERTY?

Or the more important question: why buy property right now when everyone else is renting? The reason people rent is because they are afraid of making a commitment, losing their job, and having to move to another city to find work— which is happening more now than at any other time.

The reason I am buying *now* is because most people are *not* buying now. There is less demand for houses to own, which means the prices are at an all-time low and I can grab bargain-of-the-century deals every single day. And I can secure rental income because it is so easy to find a tenant with everyone renting! Rental demand is ridiculous and driving up the cost of renting. It is simple economics: supply and demand.

I am not an economics graduate. And besides, how many economics graduates do you think are financially free? How many do you think are as wealthy as I am? Well, I can tell you, not many. Those guys are still working while I am living!

I gleaned my knowledge of property the "street way" and, most importantly, by following, subscribing to, and spending time with people who are very successful in property investment.

Now, don't get me wrong. I do not advocate property as the only investment vehicle, or as the be all and end all. Gold, for example, has done staggeringly well in the past ten years. Although it has dropped a lot recently, I predict it will come back very strong because, again, it comes down to supply and demand.

However, I like property because everybody needs somewhere to live and is prepared to pay a premium, especially if the place is well developed, has the potential for growth, and can supply a person's lifestyle needs. Yes, property is very exciting especially now, when you can buy it at below-market prices!

But before you even think about investing in property, let me offer up my blueprint's Four Ultimate Fundamentals of Property Investing:

1. You must invest at the beginning of cycles.
2. You must invest in areas where the right income-level segment of the population is growing—people who can afford the rent you need.
3. You must invest in an area where the development plan caters to the demands of the income-level segment you need to attract.
4. You must invest in an area where the economic factors are favorable—especially for entrepreneurial investment, which leads to business opportunities and job creation.

Most people are not applying these Four Ultimate Fundamentals of Property Investing, and that's why they have to keep working. It is what people are not doing that is keeping them trapped.

I am doing what other people are not because I know things other people do not know. I know the exact blueprint. I know exactly what move to make next, once the market conditions are right. I execute where other people delay. And in that execution I serve so many aces, I just keep winning and winning. And the thousands of other people who are using my blueprint are also winning every time and wondering why they didn't do it sooner!

Everybody else still working is wondering what the hell will happen next, consulting fortune-tellers and watching TV to escape the rat race of their lives. I am "watching" the life that I created—that's my channel—and I don't ever plan on taking my eyes off it, because it's exciting. I am living every moment with a purpose and without fear.

NO-MONEY-DOWN SELLER-FINANCING DEAL

Here's another normal deal I do very often and my students have followed suit. How would you like the seller of the property to finance your purchase on your terms? How would you like to make the deal a no-money-down deal? And how would you like to resell the property, receive the full sale price, and profit before you even pay for the house?

Sound impossible? No, it is very possible and happening right now.

Property: 3-bedroom, 1 bathroom, excellent condition, great suburb, existing tenant

Deposit down: $12,000 (borrowed)

Balance due in 90 days: $12,000

Renovation cost: $12,000

Sale price: $59,000

Profit: $23,000

All $59,000 received 14 days after the deposit has been paid, before the balance is due and before the renovation is paid for.

Don't tell me it can't be done, don't tell me it's difficult, don't tell me you haven't got the time. Don't tell me you haven't got the money. If I can do it anyone can, you just have to apply the blueprint.

Can you imagine doing just two of these deals per month and the difference it would make to your lifestyle? If you think it would take a long time to do a deal like this, you're wrong.

Somebody else found the deal for me and somebody else sold the property for me! All of my profit was *residual,* meaning I didn't have to do any of the work myself. I don't even live where the house is situated. I live 6,000 miles away!

Have I got your full attention now?

AUSTRALIA MINING BOOM

You'd think it couldn't get any better. Well it did.

Several years ago I secured the most incredible property deal I have seen. I discovered that in the small mining towns of Newman and Port Hedland in Western Australia the economies were off-the-charts amazing.

Why? Because some of the biggest iron ore mines in the world are based there, and the Australian mining companies were supplying China with over 155 million tons of iron ore a year to urbanize China's infrastructure. China is now 54 percent urbanized, and that percentage is expected to grow to 85 or 90 percent in the next twenty years.

So, why Australia mining towns? Simple! There was not enough housing to supply all the workers living there, and some workers had to rent rooms in ship containers for A$400 per night (about $280, seventy cents for every Australian dollar)—and even those were fully booked for two years. Other facts:

- Rents on 3-bedroom houses were A$3,000 a week!
- Truck drivers were making A$200,000 a year, and companies could not hire them fast enough.
- Towns were doubling in population every five years.

The mining boom has settled considerably, but this region of Australia is still growing in other industries and the towns' infrastructures are being heavily developed with the help of the government.

But am I buying up properties there now? No, because investment property has a governing engine, the cycle, and you must be able to forecast when the time is right to enter and right to exit. Cycles do the heavy lifting. We'll get to that later in the book.

The difference in this book is that I am going to prove everything I claim. And the people I have helped will tell you themselves. You can even meet them!

I trust now you are sufficiently excited to continue reading this book and also skeptical enough to want to inquire further for the proof to back up my claims. Knock yourself out, guys! What do you want?

Bank statements? I will happily show you originals in my office any time you request.

Remember one of the laws I gave you at the beginning? Hang out with people who have what you want and can prove they have what you want. These are the people who are qualified to give you the correct advice and influence you need to accelerate your journey to financial freedom. Whenever anyone ever tries to give you financial advice, always, always ask this question:

"Are you financially free?"

Even if they say they are, ask them to prove it. And if they cannot prove it, run from them like they have a contagious disease. Because if you stick around people like that, you will be infected with the worst financial woes of your life!

THE FINANCIAL FREEDOM GUARANTEE TEN-STEP BLUEPRINT

The ten steps below are the lessons I will teach you in the following chapters; they comprise the blueprint to your financially free future.

1. DO NOT LISTEN TO UNQUALIFIED FINANCIAL ADVICE.

If anyone you know who is not financially free is trying to give you financial advice and you listen to them, you will get exactly what they likely have: debt and hardship. Seek out truly qualified people, people who can prove they are financially free!

2. REPROGRAM YOUR DEFAULT OPERATING SYSTEM.

Recondition your mind to accept that financial success is just a learning process and that anyone can learn to be rich. This is where you activate your money brain and learn to seek out and process only qualified advice (see no. 1).

3. GET A REVOLUTIONARY, EFFECTIVE FINANCIAL EDUCATION.

You need a relevant, simple financial education you can easily learn, and you can put to use immediately (the book in your hands. Your schooling did not include any financial education program. You were not taught how to create wealth. All those years spent in school earned you the cash you have now! Happy? No, most people do not have the money they think they deserve. Now you can turn that around and start putting money in your pocket.

4. HAVE COMPELLING LIFE GOALS.

This is a something most people never think about because most people think they will never be financially free. My students create financial freedom in record time, and start doing the things they love to do, because they suddenly have the time and resources. If you do not have compelling goals, your financial freedom will be put on hold! What do you really want to do with your life?

5. MASTER PRECISE MONEY ALLOCATION.

It is not money that makes you rich; it's where you decide to invest that money. You need to allocate your money so that it gives you the best returns possible. That's how you get to create the life you've dreamed of. This is where I teach you to acquire assets that create *passive* income— that is, the assets pay you.

6. BORROW.

The science of leverage is foreign to many, yet leverage is what you have to do to create better returns that cost you less money. You will discover here that taking out the longest loan with the cheapest interest rate to acquire high yielding assets is the way to secure your financial freedom.

7. MASTER PRECISE RESEARCH ANALYSIS (PRA).

Traditional schooling doesn't teach you how to create wealth. Therefore, you haven't learned how to find the high paying assets that will replace your job forever. In this section, you will be shown how to use research and analysis to sustain your investment performance for the long term.

8. DO THE NUMBERS.

When you are ready to acquire assets that provide great returns, and you know how to spot them (because of the award-winning research tools you will have after reading this book), it's time to crunch those numbers and see which can give you the positive cash flow you need!

9. MANAGE YOUR INVESTMENTS WISELY.

Students ask me constantly, "What if I acquire an asset in another country, and a pipe bursts?" "How can I go and fix it?" Yes, you would think this is an issue and it can be if you do not know how to get your properties managed properly. Investment management can be the difference between a nightmare and a dream. Discover how it is that my properties never give me any of those problems—even though I have never seen many of them!

10. CALCULATE AND MINIMIZE YOUR RISK.

There is no reward without taking some risk. All you have to do is calculate that risk! In capturing massive wealth you must protect your gains and minimize your risk level at all times.

CHAPTER 1

DO NOT LISTEN TO
UNQUALIFIED FINANCIAL ADVICE

L et me ask you a few simple questions.

Did the government or the bank or any financial advisers, or your family or friends, advise you to buy property in the United States or United Kingdom in the very early 2000s, and to sell it in 2007? Did any of them advise you to buy gold ten years ago and sell it in 2012? Did any of these people tell you to reinvest your property profits from 2007 by buying foreclosed properties in the United States from 2008 onwards? Or to invest in new property in Singapore and London in 2009?

No?

Why do you think that is the case? Two very simple reasons: 1) Those people are not qualified because they didn't do any of that; 2) Your radar was not tuned to pick up successful financial people's strategies because you're conditioned to be an employee who must trade time for money and save hard.

Now, let me ask you another simple question. Do you think by following the simple strategies above you would have made lots of money? You are probably guessing that you would have. The truth is you could have made millions without using your own money! And you would not be reading this book right now because you would already be financially free.

The truth is some people, including myself, did follow those strategies, made millions in the process, and are still making money because we do not take advice from people who are not qualified to give it.

Do you really believe your government is great at managing money? Do you think they empower their citizens in free enterprise and money making opportunities? No? You're right. Let's take a look at some evidence.

DEBT TO GDP

GDP stands for Gross Domestic Product, which is the economic output of a country. *Debt to GDP* is the ratio of what a country owes—the debt the country is carrying or how much they are borrowing to produce all the products they export or sell within the country—to the value of everything it produces. In some countries, this ratio is greater than 100 percent! When that ratio is very high, a country has to keep borrowing to keep its infrastructure going and pay all its workers, because the tax revenue is just not enough on its own. And when this continually happens the government will do two things:

1. They will institute *austerity measures*: The Government will increase taxes and increase the cost of every service they provide so that they can collect more revenue to keep the country going.

2. They will print more money. Austerity measures do not collect enough cash. You can only collect so much money from the same amount of people paying tax; therefore, they print money.

Does that seem a bit odd to you?

They are taxing you more, and paying themselves more, so you end up with a lot less, and they end up with a lot more. It's not even your debt, yet you're paying for it and you still have to pay the people managing your tax dollars so terribly.

Let me put it this way: When you go to a supermarket and pay for your purchases you get an itemized receipt outlining exactly what you spent your money on. When you pay your tax bill the government doesn't issue an itemized receipt outlining exactly where your money went. Governments don't share that information with you because governments are not transparent. But what they do tell you is that if you don't pay your tax bill, you are breaking the law and will be jailed!

Now if you had been educated on how to understand basic economic data, you could be rich right now. If you had understood why there was an economic crisis in 2008, and you had been told to buy assets at rock bottom prices, you would be financially free right now.

GLOBAL FINANCIAL CRISIS

The world is still affected by the global financial crisis. Millions of people lost their homes and savings were wiped out in a year. The bankers gained control of the economy and the government let them do it. Home prices in some places dropped to less than half their value in as little as six months.

And I am going to take the time to explain how this happened to you. Once you understand it, first of all you're going to be so shocked at how uncomplicated it really is, and then you are going to learn for the first time in your life to be in control of your own money and stop trusting unqualified people with it.

Why did the GFC happen? How can you profit and help other people profit from every recession from now on?

Before I elaborate it is important for you to understand the definitions that follow. If you read them you will grasp what I am about to say with ease. Part of the reason I include these definitions is because you need to know the truth and you need to see that this information is the same from all sources.

INVESTMENT BANK

"An investment bank is a financial institution that assists individuals, corporations, and governments in raising financial capital by underwriting or acting as the client's agent in the issuance of securities (or both). An investment bank may also assist companies involved in mergers and acquisitions (M&A) and provide ancillary services such as market making, trading of derivatives and equity securities, and FICC services (fixed income instruments, currencies, and commodities)."

—Wikipedia, s.v. "Investment Banking," accessed October 9, 2015, https://en.wikipedia.org/wiki/Investment_banking.

DERIVATIVE

"In finance, a derivative is a contract that derives its value from the performance of another entity. This entity can be an asset, index, or interest rate, and is often called the 'underlying.' Derivatives can be used for a number of purposes, including insuring against price movements (hedging), increasing exposure to price movements for speculation or getting access to otherwise hard-to-trade assets or markets. Some of the more common derivatives include forwards, futures, options, swaps, and variations of these such as synthetic collateralized debt obligations and credit default swaps. Most derivatives are traded over-the-counter (off-exchange) or on an exchange such as the Chicago Mercantile Exchange, while most insurance contracts have developed into a separate industry. Derivatives are one of the three main categories of financial instruments, the other two being stocks (i.e., equity or shares) and debt (i.e., bonds and mortgages)."

—Wikipedia, s.v. "Derivative (Finance)," accessed October 9, 2015, https://en.wikipedia.org/wiki/Derivative_(finance).

COLLATERALIZED DEBT OBLIGATION (CDO)

"A collateralized debt obligation (CDO) is a type of structured asset-backed security (ABS). Originally developed for the corporate debt markets, over time CDOs evolved to encompass the mortgage and mortgage-backed security ('MBS') markets. Like other private label securities backed by assets, a CDO can be thought of as a promise to pay investors in a prescribed sequence, based on the cash flow the CDO collects from the pool of bonds or other assets it owns. The CDO is 'sliced' into 'tranches,' which 'catch' the cash flow of interest and principal payments in sequence based on seniority. If some loans default and the cash collected by the CDO is insufficient to pay all of its investors, those in the lowest, most 'junior' tranches suffer losses first. The last to lose payment from default are the safest, most senior tranches. Consequently, coupon payments (and interest rates) vary by tranche with the safest/most senior tranches paying the lowest rates and the lowest tranches paying the highest rates to compensate for higher default risk. As an example, a CDO might issue the following tranches in order of safeness: Senior AAA (sometimes known as 'super senior'); Junior AAA; AA; A; BBB; Residual."

—Wikipedia, s.v. "Collateralized Debt Obligation," accessed October 9, 2015, https://en.wikipedia.org/wiki/Collateralized_debt_obligation.

SUBPRIME LENDING

"In finance, subprime lending (also referred to as near-prime, non-prime, and second-chance lending) means making loans to people who may have difficulty maintaining the repayment schedule, sometimes reflecting setbacks such as unemployment, divorce, medical emergencies, etc. Historically, subprime borrowers were defined as having a FICO scores below 640, although 'this has varied over time and circumstances.'

"These loans are characterized by higher interest rates, poor quality collateral, and less favorable terms in order to compensate for higher credit risk. Many subprime loans were packaged into mortgage-backed securities (MBS) and ultimately defaulted, contributing to the financial crisis of 2007–2008.

"Proponents of subprime lending maintain that the practice extends credit to people who would otherwise not have access to the credit market. Professor Harvey S. Rosen of Princeton University explained, 'The main thing that innovations in the mortgage market have done over the past 30 years is to let in the excluded: the young, the discriminated-against, and the people without a lot of money in the bank to use for a down payment.'"

—Wikipedia, s.v. "Subprime Lending," accessed October 9, 2015, https://en.wikipedia.org/wiki/Subprime_lending.

SUBPRIME CRISIS

"The U.S. subprime mortgage crisis was a nationwide banking emergency that coincided with the U.S. recession of December 2007–June 2009. It was triggered by a large decline in home prices, leading to mortgage delinquencies and foreclosures and the devaluation of housing-related securities. Declines in residential investment preceded the recession and were followed by reductions in household spending and then business investment. Spending reductions were more significant in areas with a combination of high household debt and larger housing price declines.

"The expansion of household debt was financed with mortgage-backed securities (MBS) and collateralized debt obligations (CDO), which initially offered attractive rates of return due to the higher interest rates on the mortgages; however, the lower credit quality ultimately caused massive defaults. While elements of the crisis first became more visible during 2007, several major financial institutions collapsed in September 2008, with significant disruption in the flow of credit to businesses and consumers and the onset of a severe global recession.

"There were many causes of the crisis, with commentators assigning different levels of blame to financial institutions, regulators, credit agencies, government housing policies, and consumers, among others. A proximate cause was the rise in subprime lending. The percentage of lower-quality subprime mortgages originated during a given year rose from the historical 8% or lower range to approximately 20% from 2004 to 2006, with much higher ratios in some parts of the U.S. A high percentage of these subprime mortgages, over 90% in 2006 for example, were adjustable-rate mortgages. These two changes were part of a broader trend of lowered lending standards and higher-risk mortgage products. Further, U.S. households had become increasingly indebted, with the ratio of debt to disposable personal income rising from 77% in 1990 to 127% at the end of 2007, much of this increase mortgage-related."

—Wikipedia, s.v. "Subprime Mortgage Crisis," accessed October 9, 2015, https://en.wikipedia.org/wiki/Subprime_mortgage_crisis.

SECURITIZATION

"Securitization is the financial practice of pooling various types of contractual debt such as residential mortgages, commercial mortgages, auto loans or credit card debt obligations (or other non-debt assets which generate receivables) and selling their related cash flows to third party investors as securities, which may be described as bonds, pass-through securities, or collateralized debt obligations (CDOs). Investors are repaid from the principal and interest cash flows collected from the underlying debt and redistributed through the capital structure of the new financing. Securities backed by mortgage receivables are called mortgage-backed securities (MBS), while those backed by other types of receivables are called asset-backed securities."

—Wikipedia, s.v. "Securitization," accessed October 9, 2015, https://en.wikipedia.org/wiki/Securitization.

RATINGS AGENCY

"A credit rating agency (CRA, also called a ratings service) is a company that assigns credit ratings, which rate a debtor's ability to pay back debt by making timely interest payments and the likelihood of default. An agency may rate the creditworthiness of issuers of debt obligations, of debt instruments, and in some cases, of the servicers of the underlying debt, but not of individual consumers.

"The debt instruments rated by CRAs include government bonds, corporate bonds, CDs, municipal bonds, preferred stock, and collateralized securities, such as mortgage-backed securities and collateralized debt obligations.

"The issuers of the obligations or securities may be companies, special purpose entities, state or local governments, non-profit organizations, or sovereign nations. A credit rating facilitates the trading of securities on a secondary market. It affects the interest rate that a security pays out, with higher ratings leading to lower interest rates. Individual consumers are rated for creditworthiness not by credit rating agencies but by credit bureaus (also called consumer credit reporting agencies or credit reference agencies), which issue credit scores.

"The value of credit ratings for securities has been widely questioned. Hundreds of billions of securities given the agencies' highest ratings were downgraded to junk during the financial crisis of 2007–08. Ratings downgrades during the European sovereign debt crisis of 2010–12 have been blamed by EU officials for accelerating the crisis.

"Credit rating is a highly concentrated industry, with the two largest CRAs—Moody's Investors Service and Standard & Poor's (S&P)—controlling 80% of the global market share, and the "Big Three" credit rating agencies—Moody's, S&P, and Fitch Ratings—controlling approximately 95% of the ratings business."

—Wikipedia, s.v. "Credit Rating Agency," accessed October 9, 2015, https://en.wikipedia.org/wiki/Credit_rating_agency.

With the definitions out of the way, let's get to the really simple stuff! But please refer back to this page; it's important that these definitions get into your head. Wall Street investment bankers tell us we would never understand it. But that's basically because if we all understood it, we would *never* have let those greedy bankers dictate the world economy. But in politics money is the only language, as you will soon discover.

A SCARY TALE

Once upon a time several important people wanted to become even more important and make lots of money for themselves. One of them, a president, wanted to get re-elected and become the most popular president there ever was by enabling every American to buy their dream home.

The reason they gave for all this of course was to help the poor people, the people who couldn't get decent jobs, the people who couldn't borrow money, and the people who didn't have their own homes and wanted them so badly.

So the powers contrived a very clever idea that would make them all look good, including the President of the United States. It would make their country a powerhouse of finance, the wealthiest in the world—

trumping all the other world powers. The vision was so compelling, governments all over the world bought into the idea that this was all for the good of their citizens.

Now the very first thing these important people had to do, in case anything bad happened (which they knew would, of course), was to remove themselves from all blame. So in case the shit hit the fan, there was no way they could be prosecuted at all!

Yes, this was a clever strategy that greedy people with access to power used to success. (Well mostly, if they were smart enough and not like Jordan Belfort). In stock trading it's called a *stop loss*. However, because these people didn't play by the rules, for them there was no loss at all, only monumental gain.

And of course these very important people had to have teammates and collaborators so they could sweep the board; there was no room for error or culpability.

Now these very important people I will call the investment bankers. These investment bankers, sometime in 2000, approached the government of the United States and its president, Bill Clinton. Clinton asked them how they could help him help every American buy their dream home.

Why they approached the government had something to do with *deregulation*. What they wanted to achieve was preventing the government from snooping into their transactions and analyzing what they were doing with other people's money. They were not going for complete deregulation; oh no, they were smarter than that. They were asking to deem it *an unnecessary government regulation* that would not be required because particular trades and transactions were really low risk.

The government agreed fully to *deregulate* the trading of derivatives, which led to the biggest financial crash of all time, even bigger than the Wall Street Crash of 1929.

To make this clearer for people who don't know about derivatives, imagine you are interested in buying stock in a company to make a profit, because you have reason to believe that stock might go up in value. To buy one share in company X's stock would cost you $10. So, 1,000 shares would cost you $10,000. And if the stock increases in value your $10,000 will make a healthy profit.

However, this stock could also decrease in value and if that happened you would lose money. So here is my question: would you consider a $10,000 investment in a company you don't know much about high risk or low risk?

Well let's make this easier: if the stock price went down how much could you lose? You could lose the whole lot—all $10,000 of your investment.

So I would consider that particular investment high risk. Now you can argue about the strength of the company and that you're an experienced trader but you cannot guarantee that you will not lose a lot of your capital, because stock trading is speculative by nature. Even top traders lose more money than they win.

So how is a derivative different?

With a derivative, you do not have to buy the shares with lots of capital. What you do is buy the right to buy the share in the future, at a particular date. This is called an options trade.

You can buy the option to buy the share on May 30th at a particular price. If the price of the share goes up before the expiration date of May 30th, your option's value will increase and you can make good money with very little risk. Instead of spending $10 on one share, you can buy the option to control that share for a particular time period for, say, 30 cents.

So instead of spending $10,000 to buy 1,000 shares, you're only investing $300 to control those 1,000 shares!

Clever isn't it?

So by now you've probably have worked out that the most you can lose is only $300, and you would be correct. That is way less risky than potentially losing $10,000.

Now before this meeting with the government, derivative trades were regulated heavily, which meant the trading had to be squeaky clean and every transaction had to be scrutinized by the securities commission. Also, only certain companies could be traded this way.

The investment bankers' presentation to Clinton's government was super convincing, so convincing that the government added a caveat that the decision to deregulate could not be changed. The government saw the derivatives' lower risk, so why should they waste their time with extra manpower and costs regulating the trades?

And remember, probably most importantly, the investment bankers knew the details of Clinton's manifesto—his dream of making it possible for all Americans to live the American dream and buy their own homes! In the government's eyes, they were helping the average Joes make easier money with less risk. They really believed that! When it all fell apart in 2008, these same naïve people were like deer caught in headlights, not knowing what the hell to do and unable to avoid what inevitably became a huge financial crisis.

And when all that happened, who do you think was partying like it was 1999? Yes, you got it, the investment bankers. The government had given them the green light to do what they liked with other people's money, without regulation, and they did just that. The wolves of Wall Street had been let loose legally!

HOW IT ALL WENT DOWN

So how did the investment bankers bring about this global financial crisis?

First of all, the investment bankers will all tell you that it is too complicated and you will never understand how Wall Street works.

This stance is one that shockingly most of those bankers believe, and the ones that don't believe that, want to hide it from you, so you don't understand how they are still ripping you off! This is known popularly in the banking world as securitization (see definitions).

In a nutshell, because of deregulation, the banks, especially the sub-prime banks (you'll need to start referring back to our list of definitions now), took complete advantage by using securitization. Securitization is a way the banks could sell their mortgages as derivatives to investment bankers, who could market them as securities called CDOs.

Simplified, the banks could shift the risk of carrying their loans by selling off that risk to the investment banks. So instead of the bank taking the risk of lending you money to buy a house, and relying on you to pay it back, it didn't matter anymore, because the bank sold your mortgage to the investment bankers (and made a profit).

For example; if they loaned $100,000 to a customer, they would sell that same mortgage to the investment bankers for $150,000. And they were allowed to do this because there was no more regulation.

The investment banks then packaged them as CDOs (mostly sub-prime mortgages) and had them rated by the official rating agencies of Standard & Poor and Moody's and Fitch as AAA securities, meaning there was very little risk to them. They were deemed so low risk that the big insurance companies would insure any losses by offering a *credit default swap*. This meant if the CDO defaulted (meaning people didn't pay their mortgage payments), the insurance company would reimburse you for your loss!

Let me repeat that:

If things went badly with the CDO derivative (sub-prime mortgage) investment, the insurance company would pay for your loss, which made the investment basically risk-free.

Now, which one of you would like a totally upside, no-downside investment? Yes, correct, all of you!

The risk was perceived to be so low with these investments, that every state in the United States, bar one, and major countries all over the world *invested their pensions* with CDOs (sub-prime mortgages)! Can anyone start to see the beginning of a nightmare?

But how did this happen? Here's how:

THE THREE STEPS TO FINANCIAL RUIN

1. The government deregulated the banking system.
2. The banks invented securitization to shift away all their risk on loans.
3. All the credit rating agencies rated the CDOs AAA, because of two things: they were paid commission on each one, so it was well worth their while, and they could get away with making billions of dollars because they were not regulated; and b) they were insured by major bulletproof insurance companies like AIG who believed the credit rating agencies' ratings!

So let's break it down. Before deregulation, people with poor credit, and people who did not have any savings or regular income, could not get a loan. But after deregulation, sub-prime banks suddenly popped up to help these people buy homes.

The sub-prime banks knew they could sell any mortgage to the investment bankers because of deregulation, and they knew they could profit from this. This is how a typical conversation would have gone with a new sub-prime bank customer in 2001.

Customer: I believe this bank can give me a loan, even though I have been turned down by every other bank.
Bank: That's right, we guarantee you an approval today!
Customer: Really? I want to buy a house!

Bank: No problem, we will approve it today. How much did you want to borrow?

Customer: $250,000, is that ok?

Bank: Sure, let's workout the repayments.

Customer: Oh, I don't know if I can afford the repayments.

Bank: No problem, you can take advantage of our new teaser mortgage five-year rates. You only pay 2 percent instead of 7percent for five years, so instead of $800 a month, you only pay $250.

Customer: Wow, that's fantastic, but I don't have money for a deposit on the house.

Bank: No problem, you can borrow the deposit from us, so you pay nothing down!

Customer: Really? Wow… that's really good, but what if I want to buy furniture and renovate?

Bank: No problem at all sir, we are going to give you a 130 percent mortgage so you have all the cash you need to have the home of your dreams!

Customer: Where do I sign?

There are many of you reading this book right now thinking "No way! You're making this up." I am not. In fact, I am understating it. Can you imagine the repercussions in the economy, when everyone could buy a house without a deposit? The property markets in the United States, the United Kingdom and Australia and, many other countries, went absolutely crazy.

Housing prices started to accelerate at a rate never seen before. There was a housing development boom, there was a property boom, and there was a stock market boom. There was a credit boom. And of course there was a banking boom. Bankers were laughing all the way to the bank and all the way out of the bank—they became overnight multi-millionaires, some billionaires.

CDOs, the vehicle that contained all the unsecured sub-prime mortgages, boomed to such a degree that they became the most popular investment in history. The government and private pensions love the least amount of risk, so most invested in them not knowing they contained very dodgy sub-prime mortgages held by people with no jobs. They weren't aware because the investment bankers were not obliged to tell them. They were deregulated. Oh what a party they had!

Here's the bottom line: Don't accept financial advice from people and institutions that have demonstrated they are really awful with money and only interested in looking after their own needs, not yours.

The only way to get financial advice is by learning from somebody who is successful with money and already financially free. You need a mentor, with a successful blueprint, like the guy writing this book.

CHAPTER 2

REPROGRAM YOUR
DEFAULT OPERATING SYSTEM

T he money in your bank account right now is exactly what you deserve. Or, you could put it this way: the money in your bank account is a reflection of how you think about money. If you are not happy with the amount of money you have right now, the only way you can change that figure is by radically changing the way you think about money. Only 1 percent of the world's population thinks this other way, which is not how it should be, but that's why that 1 percent has all the wealth and you don't.

The fact is there is no mainstream education system or section on any syllabus anywhere that teaches you how to be successful with money and create wealth. You enter your adult life perfectly equipped to get into debt and totally unqualified to play the money game successfully.

You are running a default money system in your mind. Whenever you get money, you are "programmed" to lose it, and then borrow more money to buy things you don't need, to feel good about work you don't like to do.

Student debt is monumental. Many people can't pay it back until they are in their 40s. Consumer debt is toppling households into financial oblivion—an oblivion that will mean being broke when you retire.

You have been "programmed" to work for money. You only know how to be an employee and how to please people, especially your boss. Your default operating system has absolutely no skill in making money work for you; therefore you always fail at it.

In this chapter we are going to take a look at the four "programs" running inside your head that are keeping you poor, and we'll learn how to change those programs into ones that will make you rich and free.

Let's start with the brain, the first of the programs that make up your "operating system."

1. THE EVOLUTIONARY BRAIN

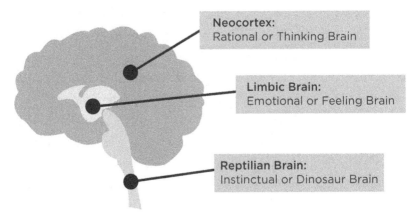

Neocortex:
Rational or Thinking Brain

Limbic Brain:
Emotional or Feeling Brain

Reptilian Brain:
Instinctual or Dinosaur Brain

As you can see, we have basically three brains within our one. The oldest of these is the reptilian brain, the brain that is there purely to help us survive. It is an instinctual, hardwired program so powerful that when we are not thinking our minds will go there immediately in reaction to any perceived threat.

Think about what a reptile has to do to survive:

- Eat
- Drink
- Keep Safe from Predators
- Reproduce

As a reptile is cold-blooded, the reptile will only move when any of those four needs are activated. The rest of the time, it will chill out. In a modern day context can you see any similarities to how a human thinks and how a reptile thinks?

Well, let me put it this way: what is the first thing you would do if you lost your job? Without exception every time I ask this question, the response is spectacularly consistent: "I would look for another job." I would not call this a response. I would call it a reaction. A response requires you to think before you answer a question, a reaction doesn't.

"I would look for another job" is a reaction to the stimulus of losing one's job or more precisely losing one's income. And when you lose your income, there is a possibility one day you will not be able to eat, because you don't have the money to pay for food. Suddenly, from the depths of your brain, at light speed, your default survival reaction kicks in: if you lose your job, you have to replace it with another one.

Why is it, when I ask that question, that no one has answered me, "I would learn how to create *passive income* so I don't have to rely on a salary anymore! That answer would be a response rather than a reaction.

You are not taught how to create passive income, nor is it hardwired into your brain. The only strategy to make money that is hardwired into your brain is generating a salary as an employee.

So anything that threatens your ability to draw a salary is perceived to be a threat to your survival. Thus, creating passive income is perceived as a threat and the knowledge you need is unwittingly blocked from ever reaching your learning center.

Your default survival system is further reinforced by the *limbic brain,* or feeling brain, the part most associated with having and rearing offspring. So it is not just one mouth you have to feed, but also your children's mouths. Losing your income becomes even more threatening.

Is it any wonder you're not wealthy when you are thinking this way?

The bottom line: you're just living off the scraps and the leftovers, you never get to the appetizer or the main course, you skip dessert, and then you go off foraging for food at bargain prices—or easy prey, just like the animals do!

The only part of the brain that separates us from animals is the *neo-cortex*, which is where the ability to rationalize thoughts and make meaning of them is generated.

The problem is you don't know how to tap into that part of the brain. It does not come with an operating manual. Your potential to grow, learn, and create lots of wealth is switched off. You have not been educated to respond and search for answers. You have been educated to remember non-relevant facts that have no power in our lives.

To give you a very good example, please answer this question: When was the last time you used a quadratic equation, Pythagoras' theorem, trigonometry, algebra, or medieval history?

I know you haven't used it, you know you haven't used it, so why the hell are we learning it and subjecting our kids to learning it? Our default system relies on references to information we have been taught to remember in school, therefore it is by default completely, utterly, bloody useless!

We can however upgrade our default operating system. We can learn to think differently. We can create wealth by learning how to find the switch that opens the gateway to overhaul our way of thinking and change our responses to every bit of new information we receive.

We can first of all learn to decode advice so we know whether it's qualified or unqualified. We can insert a new filter template that determines what information we discard and what information we focus on.

Now, as I mentioned before, the very first filter we can insert is this: Qualified financial advice originates only from qualified people who are already financially free. All other financial advice is irrelevant and should be dismissed.

Can you imagine how your life would change if this was part of your default thinking process?

Once you insert this filter, you can learn to control the gateway to your mind. You will discover that financial freedom becomes easy when the roadblocks are gone. Next, you need to understand the other three default programs running in your head, blocking your way to freedom.

2. YOUR ENCULTURATION: THE WAY YOU WERE RAISED

Let me ask you a very simple question: Were your parents rich? Or were your parents poor? If you have ever read the book *Rich Dad, Poor Dad* by Robert Kiyosaki you will know exactly what I am talking about.

How rich parents talk to children about work and money compared to how poor, working-class parents do is typically light years apart.

Even if you had rich parents but they did not take the time to sit down and educate you on how to make money, then you are still not equipped to create wealth. Indeed many children have lost their parents' fortunes because of this.

A poor parent would likely have raised you to believe that money was very hard to come by and that you have to work very hard to earn money. They would have told you that you have to go to school and study very, very hard, that you must get very high grades, and you must get into college.

You would have seen this firsthand as a child, when you realized that both your parents had to work and perhaps spend many hours away from home. You would have witnessed the stress, arguments about money, and unfortunately in many cases divorce (the lack of money being a major cause of divorce). This behavior would have been indoctrinated you into the way you "should" behave when you grow up. It would have conditioned you believe that you must also work very long hours and that arguing about money with your partner is normal.

On the other hand, your rich parent might have conditioned you to believe that you must invest and create passive income, create businesses rather than work for them, and invest profits in cash-generating assets so you never have to worry about money. Your rich parent would have had time to spend with you, would have shared many experiences with you, and showed you that you can have the time to do what you love because you don't have to be an employee.

Ninety-nine percent of you reading this book, I'm guessing, are not a product of this rich parent.

You will have to accept that you cannot carry on with the same thinking and money habits as your parents, because you will end up like them. Actually, you will be worse off than them, because pensions are disappearing and jobs that last a lifetime are non-existent.

You will have to stop using the default program that has been passed down to you.

3. YOUR SUPPORT GROUP

Who you choose to spend your time with is probably the main reason for your present financial status. For the benefit of making a point, allow me to emphasize that sentence by repeating it… Who you choose to spend your time with is probably the main reason for your present financial status.

Yes, think about it. If you are spending most of your time with people who are struggling financially who are continually using language that only reinforces the fact, how do you ever think you will grow financially? Let me put it another way. What would be the best and fastest way to learn Chinese, from a book or from spending most of your time with a Chinese family that spoke the language?

If your environment is focused on what you need to learn to succeed, you will minimize the risk of not learning it. But if you place yourself in a fertile learning environment where the only information you are exposed to is the information you need then you will definitely grow and prosper.

So if you don't like the kind of money your friends make, I highly recommend you change your friends. Let me repeat the two laws I mentioned at the beginning of this book:

1. To get what you want, you must spend most of your time with people that have got what you want.
2. To get what you want, you must remove yourself from people that have what you don't want.

Number-two is more challenging. It can be emotional; you could be married to one of these people. But remember who you choose to spend the most time with can make or break you financially.

So, as you will probably have guessed, the person you are closest to must have similar financial goals to you and must be willing to take the necessary action. This also makes for an unbelievably fantastic, flourishing relationship. Anything else will cost you time and money.

4. YOUR EDUCATION

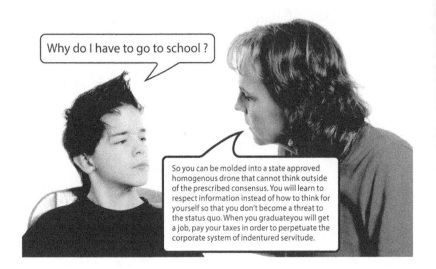

The image above really says it all. Read it and study it. The fourth default programming running in your head is your education.

When my children kept asking me why they had to go to school every day, eventually I told them the truth—that school is not going to help them find what they love to do and succeed in it.

My son, Ryker Saul Robinson, loves go-kart racing. He started when he was six and now at 14 has competed in the World Karting

Championships (qualifying 4th), and won the Kimbolton Annual Championship in the United Kingdom at his first attempt. He didn't learn this in school. His mother and I encouraged him, because he'd shown an extraordinary interest in cars since he was a baby.

For your information, karting is expensive, it costs me over £1,000 (about $1,500) a week to keep him racing. Yes he's lucky. I would never have had that opportunity at his age. I am financially free so I have been able to help my children pursue their dreams and learn about money from me. Do they appreciate it? Yes, they have learned to. They have met many underprivileged people through my charity work and love to help out themselves. I love that too.

As I have said repeatedly, a traditional school education will leave you and your children perfectly equipped to completely fail at financial freedom. The longer you spend there, the more hardwired you will become into default thinking that making money is difficult. And the end result will see you retiring destitute.

What you need is a proper qualified education in financial freedom and wealth creation. Which brings us to the next chapter …

CHAPTER 3

GET A REVOLUTIONARY, EFFECTIVE FINANCIAL EDUCATION

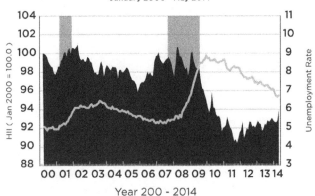

Median Household Income Index (HII) & Unemployment Rate by Month
January 2000 - May 2014

Recessionary Periods = 104*
Seasonally Adjusted Household Income Index
Monthly Unemployment Rate (seasonally adjusted)

Source: http://www.jec.senate.gov/public/index.cfm/republicans/2015
/5/breakdown-of-median-household-income-and-unemployment-rate-by-state

A huge part of achieving financial freedom is being able to decode relevant financial data that can reveal huge opportunities. Take a look at the chart above, and see if you can spot a great financial opportunity.

This chart shows two pieces of information. The line that starts on top at the left is the average household income between the years 2000 and 2014. The other line shows the monthly unemployment rate through the same years.

Most people would spot that there was significant change in these figures during 2008. Most would say, yes, unemployment rose dramatically in 2008–2009 and average income dropped a lot. And since they have read the first chapter of this book, they would say, "Oh! That's because of the global financial crisis, right?"

Well, yes it is but that's not the point. The point is to spot the financial opportunity. When an investor looks at a chart like the one above, we don't just read it… we decode it and discover untold fortunes.

For example, if I know that people's incomes are dropping dramatically and unemployment is rising dramatically at the same time, then I can conclude that not many people at that time have the confidence to buy their own house. I'd conclude that demand for property is at a low, as no one is buying. And because of the simple law of supply and demand, I would further conclude that it is highly likely home prices will drop considerably because nobody wants them.

Are you getting what I am really saying yet?

Now before I get to that, I would also conclude if I was financially educated and that if no one is buying, they must be renting! And if they are renting, rental properties must be in huge demand, which means rental prices will be going up.

So if there is likely low demand in house purchasing and there is huge demand in housing rental, is there an opportunity for me as an investor to profit? Upon further investigation I discovered property prices in some places were dropping by 60 percent in less than six months!

So I could buy a $100,000 house for only $40,000. Could it be true?

Yes it was true and I made a lot of money! The reason was because I looked at all the information, I researched the properties carefully (I will get to that in Chapter 7), and I raised the capital to buy them, so I could act swiftly and take advantage of the huge opportunity. (I will cover raising capital in Chapter 6).

People with a default employee mindset would have looked at the first chart and would have been scared to death because they would see that everybody is losing their job. Their reaction would be to go back to work and work harder! Or even get a second or third job, which thousands of white-collar workers did, many of whom ended up working in McDonald's.

The rest of us, who took the initiative of educating ourselves financially, saw opportunity and swiftly executed our financial strategies and captured below-market-value properties. It was a no brainer.

And the reason this was such a fantastic opportunity is because the rental market was going crazy. The rental yields of houses were doubling and tripling overnight. I was getting returns over 20 percent on a lot of my properties, which would have been impossible before 2008. The global financial crisis of 2008 was a perfect opportunity for the people who were fully prepared to take advantage of it.

I think you can probably start to see that the right education is extremely powerful because it can help you see things other people can't see no matter how much they stare at the same information. Your job from this day forward is to understand the language of money, and when you grasp it you can respond accordingly and take the necessary action to profit from it!

MINIMIZING YOUR RISK

Part of your new default thinking in financial education is to automatically look at risk level and assess it properly.

With regard to property in 2008, the reason I kept mentioning the rental market is because the tenants were able to reduce my risk greatly as they pay me enough money to service the mortgage. Not only that, because the rental income was so high compared to the cost of the house, the rent more than covered the mortgage. It gave me positive cash flow.

Let's look at the numbers with an example, a house I bought for $50,000:

House Cost: $50,000
Monthly mortgage payment: $300
Monthly rent paid by tenant: $600

From the breakdown you can see I am collecting $300 in cash every month even though I took a loan to buy the house. That $300 is passive income and this extra money in your pocket can start to replace your salary. The more property you are able to acquire, the more passive income you will create, and the faster you will reach financial freedom!

Can you reduce your risk any further? That's a great question, and believe it or not, yes you can! Because rental demand is very high in certain areas and unemployment is still high, to help its citizens there are certain governments, such as the United Kingdom and the United States that will pay welfare to certain individuals, including paying 100 percent of their rent. In the United States they call this welfare program *Section 8:*

Section 8 of the Housing Act of 1937 (42 U.S.C. § 1437f), often called Section 8, as repeatedly amended, authorizes the payment of rental housing assistance to private landlords on behalf of approximately 4.8 million low-income households as of 2008 in the United States. The largest part of the section is the Housing Choice Voucher Program, which pays a large portion of the rents and utilities of about 2.1 million households. The U.S. Department of Housing and Urban Development manages the Section 8 programs.

—Wikipedia, s.v. "Section 8 (Housing)," accessed October 9, 2015, https://en.wikipedia.org/wiki/Section_8_(housing).

Approximately 20 percent of the property that I own in the United States has Section 8 tenants. Am I happy? Yes! Because I get paid on time by the government. Now, some of you may be thinking my welfare tenants are not the best tenants to have, that they are more risky because they might damage the property. I understand your thinking on that; however, there is another risk mitigation strategy.

If your Section 8 tenant damages your property once, they are not allowed to claim the Section 8 benefit again for the rest of their lives. The penalties are severe for any abuse of the benefit and because of this my Section 8 tenants take very good care of my property.

As many of you read this, I am sure jaws are dropping at what you simply did not know was possible. And why they didn't teach this in school!

I am not just talking to Americans. I do not live in the United States but I own lots of property there because there are no restrictions on foreign ownership. However, I also own a lot of property in the United Kingdom, Australia, Singapore, Malaysia, and Cambodia. I do not only focus on one market, I focus on the markets that give the best returns at the right time. I buy by studying property cycles all over the world, which is one of the four cornerstones of acquiring great wealth through property investing.

THE FOUR ULTIMATE FUNDAMENTALS OF PROPERTY INVESTING

Now that we've touched on the basics of decoding financial data and minimizing risk, I'm going to give you the four principles of your financial freedom education that you must master to be thoroughly financially free.

1. Always invest at the beginning of a **real estate cycle.**
2. Make sure the **population** of the suburb is growing and understand why it is.
3. Study the construction **development plan** of the suburb and confirm that massive investing is going on so that people will stay there and others will be attracted to moving there.
4. Make sure all **economic factors** are favorable. Employment opportunities in the area should be abundant and likely to be abundant for a long time to come. Make sure it is easy for companies and entrepreneurs to do business there, and that you have a friendly local government.

Let's look at each principle in detail.

1. Master the Global Economic Cycles of Property.

When you learn that all property markets have a cycle, meaning there are peaks, corrections, beginnings, and middles, you can start pinpointing great opportunities in different markets. When a country starts do to well financially, its economy starts to perform, it's GDP to Debt ratio starts increasing (meaning debt decreases and profits soar), directly benefitting the property and stock markets.

What I am going to do now is paraphrase from my friend Paul Counsel, Ph.D. It was from Paul that I learned all about property cycles, who became a multi-millionaire within a few years after mastering this knowledge—which again is not taught in any school!

One of the first ever people to notice property cycles was a gentleman named Homer Hoyt. He studied a 100-year period of land prices in the city of Chicago, and observed that cycles were never shorter than 17 years and never longer than 21 years and averaged 18 years.

Hoyt observed that property cycles follow a predictable pattern, as sure as night following day. It's a pattern of three distinct phases: boom ... slump ... recovery ... and then a new boom phase can commence.

History reveals that turning points in economic cycles are generally marked by the collapse or near collapse of a major bank that has overstretched and put itself at the mercy of rising interest rates and expensive funding, while chasing more growth.

All recovery phases begin at the bottom of a cycle, which is characterized by cheaper land and lower interest rates. These conditions allow production to expand and business confidence to return to market conditions.

As a result of improvement in economic activity, demand for land increases. As land values increase, speculators hold out for opportunities to capture future economic rent increases.

Let me define *economic rent*: "An excess payment made to or for a factor of production over and above the amount expected by its owner. Economic rent is the positive difference between the actual payment made for a factor of production (such as land, labor or capital) to its owner and the payment level expected by the owner, due to its exclusivity or scarcity." —Investopedia, s.v. "Economic Rent," accessed October 9, 2015, http://www.investopedia.com/terms/e/economicrent.asp.

So the more rare a property you buy, the more demand it attracts and creates opportunity for gains above your expected payment. (In Chapter 7, I will explain how you do this.)

At cycle peaks, everything appears rosiest, and competition to produce the world's tallest building is at its highest. The world's tallest buildings have a history of being completed at cycle peaks.

Tallest building on Earth

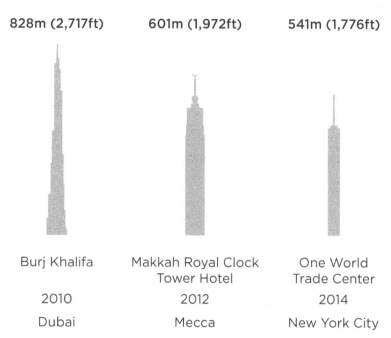

828m (2,717ft)	601m (1,972ft)	541m (1,776ft)
Burj Khalifa	Makkah Royal Clock Tower Hotel	One World Trade Center
2010	2012	2014
Dubai	Mecca	New York City

Source: http://www.ctbuh.org/TallBuildings/HeightStatistics/tabid/1735/language/en-US/Default.aspx

Because commercial skyscrapers are speculative projects, they are a sure sign of easing credit conditions. It's important to watch the relationship between credit availability and speculator activity, because it's the credit created by banks that fuels property cycles. You have to understand how the availability of credit impacts the increased availability of land and how it impacts the investor speculation that leads to price increases.

Banks Love Creating Credit

Credit growth fuels bank profitability. Banks not only create credit, they create indebtedness and mortgages as well. This is the fundamental reason property cycles happen and why they go through boom and bust phases. Because every dollar that's created comes into existence through debt—i.e., it's borrowed into existence. The banks ultimately end up controlling the activities of workers.

A society based on indebtedness is a society that's engineered to work, not for itself and its future but for the banks and their futures. Banks are always on the lookout for ways to increase their profit through indebtedness.

Always try and observe how and when this takes place in any given property cycle. Bankers own the earth; take it away from them, but leave them with the power to create credit, and with the stroke of a pen they will create enough money to buy it back again!

If you want to be slaves to the bankers and pay the cost of your own slavery, then let the banks create money.

Unless you are strategic about how you borrow money, once you borrow money for unproductive purposes, you unwittingly surrender a degree of your freedom to your creditor.

And the epitome of unproductive purposes is the consumer frenzy known as "retail therapy." People borrow to buy branded goods to feel and look good. This only creates debt and this habit creates more slavery, as you have to pay it back. Investing is different because you get a return. The fundamental law I will repeat here is: *Rich people invest first and spend what they have got left. Poor people spend first and save what they have got left* (which in 98 percent of cases is very little and the interest given on savings is obscenely low, it won't even cover inflation.)

A New Cycle

Property developers begin building when interest rates are low, because they can borrow money cheaply and then other people can buy the property they build because they also can get cheaper loans! Property increases in value the longer banks keep the interest rates low and make borrowing easy. One way they make borrowing easy is allowing very low deposits, such as 10 percent down to buy a house. So the bank would loan you 90 percent of the price of the house. (Before the financial crisis, you could get a 130 percent, which is why house sales exploded.)

When land prices go up, property developers don't want to buy more land; instead, they want to build more floors onto buildings that are on the land they already own. With more square footage, they can get more profit from their buildings. This is why the world's tallest buildings are so often completed when land prices are at a peak. If land prices always stayed the same, there would not be as many skyscrapers.

Another indicator of an approaching peak in a particular real estate cycle is the price of copper. Since copper is needed in many areas of construction, copper prices have a history of spiking to new highs as we approach the peak of the cycle. Economic activity becomes frenetic.

After interest rates reach their highest point in a cycle, the slump begins. It's almost always coupled with an event that causes a loss of confidence, such as the collapse of a bank. For example, in 2008 when Lehman Brothers collapsed, it caused a huge loss in confidence in the whole global economy. Those who get wiped out are those who highly leverage themselves around the time a cycle peaks. Real wealth is created by leveraging yourself at the beginning of cycles and using that cash flow to manage credit from peak to peak, so you are never in a position of not being able to pay your monthly bills. This gives you the greatest opportunity to capture passive income from your rental properties. And in a recession you are protected. In recessions most things are cheaper, too, which is even more good news, because you have buying power and can grab lots of bargains.

As economic pressure expands to developing nations, the greater the global impact of the boom and slump nature of real estate cycles. Because the past repeats itself, we can predict the future.

Despite the gloomy news that's currently feeding the media, it's important to understand that real estate cycles over the past 214 years have continually repeated themselves and current conditions suggest future repeats. Research by Economic Indicator Services Founder Phillip J. Anderson concludes that the various phases of each economic cycle produce reliable eighteen-year property cycles, confirming what Homer Hoyt said. Peak to bottom to flattening out generally occupies the first four years of a new cycle. The remaining fourteen years contain growth phases, with boom conditions occupying the last two of the eighteen years, and the beginning of the next cycle. Anderson argues that the reason for the eighteen-year cycle can be found in historical long-term interest rates of 5 percent.

Fourteen years is the amount of time it takes for a sum of money to double in value through the effects of compounding, at a 5 percent interest rate. Historically, it's also the average amount of time it took for the majority of homeowners to raise enough cash to buy their own home.

I am betting you have never been that close to knowing that much about property cycles! Learning and relearning that information has served me very well—so well that I have consistently been able to predict property cycles for the last fifteen years, in some cases so accurately that I have made my students millions of dollars by advising them when to buy, when to refinance, and when to sell.

A Note About Compounding Your Assets

What is compounding? Well, Albert Einstein called compound interest the greatest miracle of all. Why? Because he studied how money grew when you calculated the effects of interest paid on interest cumulatively over time. For example, if I told you to take one dollar and double it, then double that the next day, and keep doubling every day for the next thirty days, how many dollars would you have on the thirtieth day?

Not one person I've asked has ever gotten the answer right. The answer is gobsmacking: the cumulative effect of doubling your dollar every day adds up to nine figures in thirty days (2, 4, 8, 16, 32, 64, 128, 256, 512, 1024, 2056, etc.). That's how compound interest works.

2. Master the Markers of Population Growth.

This is really the one principle that increases rents and values the fastest because it closely follows the simple rule of supply and demand. If you buy a house in a suburb and you charge a rent of $1,000 per month but the average income of the population is only $1,000 per month, you have a big problem.

Population growth is important, but a population with the appropriate income stream with which to buy or rent your property is far more valuable. On the other hand, if there's not enough supply of housing that the population can afford and matches their lifestyle, prices will be driven up dramatically.

And here's a good example of this:

As I mentioned earlier, due to the mining boom in Australia— driven by China's demand for iron ore—property prices in small mining towns accelerated more than in any other region in the world. And because of the undersupply of decent housing for miners, the rents went crazy. So much so that many workers in those towns had to fly in daily to get to work.

I own property in these towns, such as Port Hedland and Newman, and the rents have been as high as A$3,000 (about $2100) per week for a three bedroom house. The houses were worth about A$700,000 or A$800,000. The yield was about 15 percent-plus. This kind of rental income is just not available anywhere else in the world for that kind of investment.

And now you can begin to see that if you had purchased one of those houses (yes, just one), and even if you had a 90 percent mortgage on the property, you would clear A$6,500 net. And that is how you attain financial freedom!

A$6,500 per month is a lot of money, way more than the average monthly salary across the world. It's the kind of money that would help you leave a job you don't like and start to do the things you love to do with your life. Many friends of mine quit their jobs because of this fantastic opportunity.

This is the best example of population growth increasing your asset values that I can give, but population growth is not exclusive to this region. It can happen anywhere in the world and when you can predict where it will take place then you will be able to capitalize on profits and income.

For example, not a lot of people know that the UK town of Manchester has grown in population by over 20 percent in the past decade or so. Not a lot of people know that the Hispanic population in the United States has grown over 40 percent in the past fifteen years. I own properties in both Manchester and across the United States, and I am earning great yields because I go where the population is growing and where they can afford my property.

It really baffles me why there is such a mystery about making lots of money and ensuring your financial security. This really is not difficult at all. Imagine a world in which you learned everything I am sharing with you now at school. People like me would not exist, because you would already be rich.

3. Master Researching Development Plans.

This is one of those areas people miss all the time, but simply put, if they are developing the area you are investing in the right ways, then more people will be attracted to the place.

A great development plan should have the following:

- Significant shopping outlets and convenience services, such as dry cleaning, take-out food, car washes, etc.
- A good selection of restaurants and entertainment.
- An advanced transportation system easily accessible via rail, bus, and road, especially the central business district.
- A nice environment, with parks and lots of greenery.
- Advanced education facilities.
- Plenty of community centers for relaxation where people can meet similar-minded people.
- Culture and places of historic interest that are relevant and of interest to the population.
- And of course, great housing and smart zoning (meaning the industrial and commercial centers are not next door to each other).

If a town or city is not investing in infrastructure it is not going to attract better people, it really is that simple. If it is an old area that is not investing in rejuvenation it is not going to attract better people. And if the area is not attracting new businesses, it's not going to generate jobs and people will leave. The primary reason people leave an area is because of a lack of employment, which brings me to the last principle, or cornerstone, of acquiring great wealth.

4. Master the Economic Factors.

Property prices increase when more jobs are created in an area, because people will move there for these jobs. If housing is made affordable in the area where more jobs are being created, people won't have to travel from their original locations. They will be tempted to rent in the new area and even buy.

A great example of this is the US city of Indianapolis, Indiana. When the global financial crisis of 2008 hit the United States, a lot of people lost their jobs and could not afford to keep their homes. Indianapolis started to thrive again, offering thousands of new jobs in the pharmaceutical and car industries.

Carmel, a suburb of Indianapolis, was recently voted one of the best suburbs in the whole of the United States. The Indianapolis area has reasonable property taxes and, another plus for real estate investing, if you need to evict non-paying tenants it takes only two weeks after they're one month late. In some states it takes over six months.

So, important economic factors include job creation, business investment, and also friendly local government.

In Manchester, England, a Chinese construction firm has invested £800 million to turn the airport into Manchester Airport City. The Chinese are making Manchester a European hub so their exports can reach more people—and by the way the Chinese are rich as hell! It is by far the richest country in the world, as they simply have no debt.

And if that wasn't enough, the Abu Dhabi group that owns Manchester City Football Club is investing another £1 billion in rejuvenating the residential housing areas in central Manchester, offering first-time buyers deals on homes. First-time buyers move property markets—when they can get credit. And as the UK government has introduced a new, first-time buyer, housing incentive program, which only requires a 5 percent deposit on a first home, you can imagine how that has helped boost Manchester property prices considerably.

And if that wasn't enough, the UK government has just thrown another £600 million into its Northern Hub project, which will improve the rail system in the north of England, allowing hundreds more trains to run each day.

That is why currently I love Manchester. The investment in the infrastructure from all directions is making it one of the hottest property investment areas in the world. I am sharing this not to sell you property in Manchester but to showcase an example of all our fundamentals working in harmony.

Part of my conditioning is to always have my radar focused on for these four fundamentals. When I see any of the fundamentals changing in any given area, my default programming says, "Look for further information." As soon as I reach a critical mass of favorable fundamentals, I make a site visit and validate my research. This has made me millions of dollars and created financial freedom for thousands of my students and clients.

Sadly, most of the world is not focused on this and that's one reason why it's been predicted that in 2016 the richest 1 percent will own more than 50 percent of the world's wealth (*The Guardian,* http://www.theguardian.com/business/2015/jan/19/global-wealth-oxfam-inequality-davos-economic-summit-switzerland, accessed October 2, 2015).

Now you know why 99 percent of the world retires broke. And now I hope you are starting to learn that you can prevent that with the proper financial education from a qualified financial freedom expert.

CHAPTER 4
HAVE COMPELLING LIFE GOALS

By far the biggest reason people never become financially free is because they don't know what they would do with the time they would have if they stopped working. This is something most people never think about because most people think they will never be financially free.

My students create financial freedom in record time and start doing the things they love to do, because they have the time and resources to do them. If you do not have compelling goals, your financial freedom will be put on hold. What do you really want to do with your life? Create your goals now!

I cannot emphasize it enough: if you do not know how you really want to spend your time, you will go backwards and spend your time doing what you have been conditioned to and what you are used to. You will go back to work. You need to have *compelling life goals*. These goals must be compelling enough that they're all you think about doing when you have the free time.

When you are working, all you think about is work, because you have to do it every day and earn enough money to pay your bills. But when you're not working, you can dream about doing the things you love. That dream does not seem within reach, because you simply believe you will never have the time or money to do it. Therefore, you don't move toward achieving those dreams—you dismiss them as soon as you get up and go to work.

HOW TO DISCOVER WHAT YOU REALLY WANT

This step in the blueprint has been the most challenging for many of my students, as people are so conditioned to think they will never achieve their dreams. It's going to take plenty of practice to master this step. But master it you must!

To help you do this, I have written some questions down that you can ask yourself to help you understand what you really want to do with your time—really, what your purpose is.

- What would you love to do more of?
- What would you love to learn?
- Where would you love to go?
- Who would you love to connect with?
- What would you love to achieve?
- What would you love to contribute?

One answer I hear from everyone I have worked with is: "see more of my friends and family." It's a great answer, except that your friends and family will be working! So when you call them at 3 p.m. from some coffee shop in a beautiful location and ask them to come hang out they will tell you, "Mmmh...would love to but I have to work."

After hearing this again and again, you may start to think, "Have I done the right thing here?" If you are single and not sharing your new freedom with anyone, you are going to start to feel very lonely. In fact, some people feel so lonely they end up going back to work.

So now you can appreciate your predicament and see that you have to start hanging out with new friends who are financially free. Of course, there are new communities to be found that have the same mindset as you and me, and we do hang out and have a lot of fun.

FULFILLING YOUR HIGHEST NEEDS

When I ask what you would love to do more of, I am really asking you what you want to do for yourself. There are so many things you can be doing, and the amazing thing is, when you start doing what you really love to do, you lose all sense of time and it feels wonderful. Some people get this from fishing, sports, hobbies—like collecting antiques and selling them for a profit—some people get it from reading, writing, or traveling. Even starting a new business you have always dreamed about. That's I what I love to do more of the most.

The point is you now you have time. Because you have insured your income through the generation of passive income and replacing your salary, you now have the license to do whatever the hell you want!

The reason I chose the six questions I did is because they relate to what your soul is yearning for, what you need to feel truly fulfilled. When Abraham Maslow created his hierarchy of human needs in the 1940s (see graphic **below**), he discovered that *self-actualization* is the ultimate human state. This is the state you are in when everything in your life is in harmony, you have found your purpose, and are achieving your goals. Simply put, you are living your dream on a daily basis. You are doing this because you are not spending your time worrying about your lowest needs, the basics needed for survival. You're not worrying because you are financially free and have shifted your focus to higher needs. That transition at first may be difficult; however, when you start living every day without worrying at all about survival, that's when you really start living!

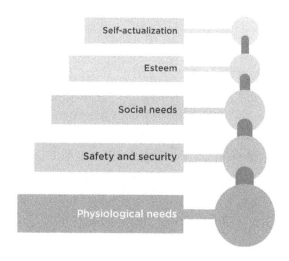

Maslow's hierarchy lists the following five levels of needs:

1. Physiological needs. This level of needs deals with the basic necessities of human survival like food, clothing, and shelter. If a person does not fulfill these needs he or she will cease to function.
2. Safety and security. Once the first level needs are met, a person feels the need to have safety in all aspects of life ensured.
3. Social needs. This deals with the innate need to feel as if one belongs in a chosen social or family group and in various other relationships. There is a need to be accepted; in the absence of belonging and acceptance, people are prone to negative effects like depression and loneliness.
4. Esteem. This level is the need to feel good about oneself and to get recognition from others. A lack of esteem will result in feelings of inferiority and helplessness.

5. Self-actualization. To become self-actualized is to become the best one can be. This is the need is to maximize one's potential.

Now I will add one more level to this hierarchy. At the top of the hierarchy, just as Tony Robbins discovered and shares so well, is the need to *grow and contribute.*

Indeed, if you think about it, helping underprivileged and unfortunate people better themselves is the most rewarding and fulfilling thing you could ever do. You are directly changing people's lives forever, and it is you, and only you, doing this.

The gratification you receive from helping people in need is extremely emotional. It brings an overwhelming sense of happiness, as if you've you truly awakened your human spirit. When you feel this self-actualization and you are able to grow and contribute, you'll be amazed to see there are really no limits, no doubts anymore. All your focus is on what you can do, not what you can't do.

And please note with utmost regard, you can really only do this when you are financially free. And that is what you must focus on now if you want the kind of life we are talking about.

It is now time to start visualizing what you want to do with your life as much as you can. It is time to get ready and prepare yourself for a life without a job. It is time to start believing you can have the life you want.

To do that, pose those six questions to yourself on a daily basis, and you will get the answers. When you do, hold on to those thoughts. Keep a notebook with you at all times and write them down, because the only person that can design your life is you. Currently, you have left it in the hands of fate. There is no fate, there is only direct action creating a direct consequence.

CHAPTER 5
MASTER PRECISE MONEY ALLOCATION

W e start this process by looking in detail at your net worth to see where you stand currently. A higher net worth will allow you to acquire more assets that pay you an income.

Some of you who are reading this book and completing this net worth exercise won't be happy; some of you are going to have a negative net worth, some of you are going to start to cry. Before you do that, please understand that your net worth can improve considerably in a very short time when you know how to allocate your money precisely.

Precise money allocation (where you actually put your money) is critical in creating wealth and financial freedom. Most people put it in entirely the wrong places, and they also decide to lock that money away for years in unproductive pensions and life insurance schemes.

Let me tell you something very important. Pensions and life insurance have been the worse performing investments ever. And in most cases, they have produced negative returns; so much so that governments of major welfare countries have increased retirement ages simply because they don't have enough money in the pensions to pay what they should.

The UK government implemented a ruling in April 2015 that allows individuals to access their pensions as of age 55, with a lesser early withdrawal tax penalty than they would otherwise be subject to. What did I say in step one of my blueprint? Never listen to government or any other unqualified advice. As you can see, this ruling is a prime example of government's mismanagement of money.

In America, as I related and shared in chapter 2, because of deregulation and government ignorance, Americans saw huge losses in their retirement funds in 2009—of those with $200,000 or more, average losses were greater than 50% percent—and have never regained their value. How would you feel if you were retiring at sixty-five and half of your pension was gone, having been abused by greedy bankers and an ignorant government?

These stories are not exclusive to the United Kingdom and the United States; Australia's retirement funds are just as bad, giving incredibly bad returns. Asian countries, such as Singapore, are giving a measly 2.5 percent per year, on average, for their CPF pension funds. It does not pay to contribute to a pension and work all your life to keep doing it. You are not in control at all.

And if you still doubt what I am sharing here, think very carefully about what I mentioned before: When you pay your taxes does the government give you an itemized receipt (like a supermarket receipt) listing how your tax money was allocated? No way!

If you think about it, it doesn't take a genius to figure out why that is the case. Every government in the world is completely non-transparent, which means that every government will use your tax dollars however they want—including spending billions in marketing campaigns to spread a veneer so thick you become numb and pay your taxes nevertheless.

So now, since you don't know how your government allocates your tax money, it's time that you managed your own money and put it in the places that will give you the best returns.

As I mentioned in detail earlier; your conditioning since childhood, as well as whom you hang around with and so on, has determined the way you are with money. And if you haven't got the money to do whatever you want instead of having to work, then you are clueless with a capital "C."

So let's get down to it, what is net worth all about? It is about tracking what your money is doing. What you must understand with complete clarity is whether your money is doing something with or without your effort. *Is your money working for you, or are you working for your money?*

As I have already shared with you, 98 percent of the world's population is working for their money, and they have to keep working because the money they earn does not give them any return at all. In most cases if you factor in inflation (the continual rise in the cost of living) it gives a minus return. Then you get into debt because you cannot afford a decent lifestyle with just your salary, so you have to borrow to buy nice things to make you feel decent, like big TVs, nice cars, new kitchens, designer clothes, and so on. What it boils down to is that you become fantastic at spending.

Ninety-eight percent of people in the world have the mastered the art of spending and debt creation, while 2 percent have mastered the art of financial freedom and wealth creation. This may be the first time you have even heard the term "net worth," let alone sat down and really "counted your money" and thought about where it really is and what it's really doing.

The first thing you need to focus on is your *assets,* or things you own that appreciate in value. One thing I must point out here is that cars do not appreciate. Most beginners of this exercise list their car as an asset. It is only an asset when you can sell it and get cash out of the sale.

Of course there are exceptions. If you have a 1964 Ferrari 250 GTO California resting in your garage, you have an asset, because it is rare and a collectible. Of course there might be some cash in your car, if you have paid off some of your loan or bought it with cash, but that money could have been used for other things.

Working out your net worth really tells you where you are, cash-wise, right now. It does not tell you how to invest your money. It just gives you a score, which is important because this score goes a long way in determining how much you can borrow, or leverage. What you need to learn is this: generally and in most cases, you cannot be financially free unless you borrow!

The thing is, you think nothing about borrowing on your credit card and buying crap with it that will never appreciate. What most people cannot get their head around is borrowing to make money!

And you will see this is the major, critical success factor that all rich people, even people that are just starting to make money, have learned well. They have learned to borrow to buy the right assets that pay them an income. Because they have chosen the right assets, they have minimized their risk substantially, they have created more income than debt, and they have guaranteed themselves financial freedom.

If we discount inherited money and lottery wins, all of those rich people started from zero, and in most cases started in debt—including me. I was a million dollars in debt. If you were a million dollars in debt, would you ever dream one day you would be rich and successful without any money worries?

Well at several points I didn't either until I found my belief, found a mentor, discovered and mastered the blueprint I am sharing with you in this book, and started spending my time hanging with other rich and successful people. Getting rid of the losers in my life was at first very difficult, but then I even mastered that. I got better and better at spending less time with the wrong people, I began to recognize their traits, characteristics, and language patterns, I began to spot them a mile off, and I learned the freedom of choice.

I chose to be successful and really freaking good with money. And once I made that choice with absolute certainty I made $12 million in a year. I ain't going back to hanging with losers; I think you can see why.

Now have a look at the net worth calculator form on page 58, or download a bigger version here: www.financialfreedomguarantee.com/networth. You will see I have created categories for all your assets (money you have) and liabilities (money you owe). We'll begin with assets.

ASSETS

1. Cash—Checking/Savings/Life Insurance surrender value/Other cash (in jars, under the bed, etc.)

This represents basically all the cash you have in hand, bank accounts, any savings, even your life insurance surrender value has some cash in it, and I would strongly advise you to cash that in, as the returns you have been getting will make you want to throw up.

2. Investments—Stock/Bonds/Derivatives/Mutual funds

Most of you reading this book will not have investments like this, but a surprising number of you will have stock that you've left in the stock market for months and even years without having a clue what it is doing. Most stock will go up eventually, but sadly most of you will lose this way, because you have not mastered the skill of stock investing or share trading yet. My advice? Get it out of there, and put it where you know it will make you money because you have learned how to do that.

3. Property—Real estate (market value)/Car (present value)/Silver, gold bullion/Fine jewelry/Art/Stamps/Coins/Collectibles, etc./Any other property of value

This covers the property you own right now. I have not included investment property yet. Most people consider the property they live in to be their home, not really an asset; however, you can certainly begin to think about how you can leverage that home to create more income from the equity you have in it.

In terms of gold, a lot of people jumped onto that bandwagon during the 2008 crash, and gold has rocketed in the last 15 years. However since 2012, it has dropped nearly 40 percent. Most people still own the gold they bought in 2012 hoping and praying for an increase. But if they were financially educated, they would have known that gold also works in very clear cycles, just like the property cycles I've been talking about. The uninformed buy at the crazy peaks, afraid all the gold will be bought up, instead of considering the cycles.

4. Investment Property—Real estate that provides income (and gives you *positive cash flow*, replacing the need for a salary or a job!)

I have now mentioned on numerous occasions that when you find these golden nugget properties, you will never worry about money again. The question remains how to find them.

But when you do, decent rental properties will give you 12 percent-plus annual returns every month, month in and month out. So if you managed to acquire a $50,000 house, that would create $6,000 per year of income you never had before. When you start buying more of those, you don't need to work ever again. I hope I am driving home the point here!

So list any investment property that is giving you an income. If it's not giving you an income, unless you are already financially free, this is going to give you a big headache and possible risk of bankruptcy. (I will be sharing how to find the best investment property in chapter 7, but please do not skip chapter 6, as that is one of the most important in the whole book and something you must absolutely master!)

5. Retirement and Pension Funds—401(k)s, IRAs, company pensions

Most people have no clue how much is in their retirement fund, and they most certainly do not know what return they're getting. What I can tell you most assuredly is this: your retirement fund money is not working for you.

If we look at the United States, most people start getting distributions from their 401(k)s around age 65. The average total value of 401(k)s after the global financial crisis was $61,000, which represented a 60 percent decrease from the previous year. How the hell are you supposed to live on that for the rest of your life? Even if it's double or triple that amount, most people spend their entire retirement savings within three years of retiring! Retirement Plans now in the USA are returning 3 to 4% per annum! But keep reading, because I am going to show you how you can make 20%++ from your pension in this Book without spending any money. You will be absolutely blown away!

You can invest your Retirement Fund into Property, which can return you between 10% and 25% per annum!!!!

There are things you can do with your retirement money before you claim it; you are allowed to withdraw funds to make a deposit on a property—amazingly, most people do not know this. In the United Kingdom, you can withdraw your retirement money and reinvest it privately, as you like, even in property. This is fantastic news, especially if you have finished reading this book and are ready to apply the strategies within it. The results will blow your mind.

So, please, find out how much your retirement fund has in it, do the research on how you can use it, and it can be a great asset you can use right now.

Next we need to look into your liabilities in order to have a true picture of your net worth and the money you have available. I am going to break it down for you here, so you have clarity as to what it is costing you to hold your assets and maintain your existing lifestyle.

It is time to accept some pain and add up your debts. It is not time to panic—addressing your debt is easier than you think!

If you decide to educate yourself further, there are opportunities for one-on-one coaching, where your debt can be consolidated and reduced massively. This way, you can increase your net worth and acquire more assets that pay you an income. This must be your primary objective, as soon as you have finished reading this book.

There is good debt, by the way—this is the debt you use to accumulate assets that pay you cash every month. Even though you are servicing a loan, there's cash above and beyond that loan payment, which will eventually replace your salary so you can start doing the things you want to do with your life … finally!

LIABILITIES

1. Automobile Loan

Contact the finance company or bank holding your loan and ask for the payoff amount. Put that on the correct line of your net worth form. Please note for future reference that cars can be refinanced or sold. If comes down to it and you really want that cash, you can use public transportation for a while; short-term pain can have an awesome, long-term gain!

2. Credit Card Debt

Welcome to everybody's debt world. For most people, by far the most debt they carry is credit card debt. It is the easiest credit to get, easiest debt to accumulate, and the most expensive. With most cards, on average you are paying 20 percent interest per year. Because they are so convenient to use, the debt and the interest just pile up, sometimes before you know it, you're in a dark place where it feels like you will never pay off the balance.

Get the balances on all your cards and put the total into your net worth calculator. We can strategize how to get rid of this debt and use your cards for financial leverage later. They may come in handy—allowing you to use them to put a deposit down on your next property purchase (and still have positive cash flow). Yes, it can be done! And it can be great fun and very satisfying.

3. Property Mortgages

This is the best debt. Simply call the bank or mortgage company, get your mortgage statement emailed to you, and you'll know the balance—the amount you still owe on your house. One of the most exciting things about home mortgages is that you can refinance at a cheaper rate with a longer term, giving your financial freedom goal a huge kick in the right direction, which I will share more about later.

But first you have to know some truths about the real estate you are carrying: is the property you have that mortgage on worth keeping, and is it giving you enough return to justify the debt? If you're not sure, don't worry; this is something that you will have complete clarity on by the end of this book!

4. Student Loans

Coming a close second to credit card debt is student loan debt, something I classify as one of the most widespread con jobs in existence. That's because it is money spent that creates no return, all it does is give you a degree that may help you get a job in an impossible job market with massive competition.

A forty-year-old friend I have in Los Angeles recently had $180,000 in student loan debt, money he borrowed to go to law school. He became a lawyer and promptly quit, because he hated it. Now he is an assistant Script Writer on a top TV show, which he loves; however, because his debt is so high, he lives with constant stress and money problems.

You know my feelings and the facts I shared about traditional education. It really is useless if you want to make a lot of money, or even get any returns on money you have. Please educate your own kids about money. My daughter just purchased her first house at 18, my son is now looking at one at 14! Imagine if you had a dad that educated you about property investment and financial freedom. Well, you would not be reading this book!

These really are the four main liability areas you need to focus on and learn to engineer into great debt that gives you a great lifestyle.

In the next chapter we are going to see how we can use your net worth to start building your financial freedom right away. I hope you are just as excited as I am writing this. When I first learned what I have just explained to you, I could not wait to get started. And I began getting results that I would have never have imagined, even though I started quite late at 34.

Even in the past ten months I have acquired four property developments (ninety-six apartments in all) in Manchester worth nearly £9 million (about $14 million), making a profit of £3 million and generating a rental income of over £70,000 a month!

You can view all of my properties by visiting this link: **http:// freedominvestor.com**

I used other people's money to finance the deposits and bridge-loaned (a short-term loan I can get approved instantly without applying to a bank) the balances. Three of those properties cost me less than £1 million each. One cost me £4 Million. Now I have just refinanced one, which has given me another £500,000 to invest in whatever I fancy. Most likely I will invest that in my next property development, as the cycle is hot right now, and values are increasing rapidly. (Remember what I told you about property cycles? Get in at the beginning! Let the cycle do the heavy lifting!)

I never thought any of this was possible before but now it's normal. Imagine what you could do if you were executing similar strategies. And if you are wondering how I used other people's money to raise the deposits, I created my own crowd-fund company. We pay a return to anybody who invests with us and give that person a share of the property.

This is not a sales pitch—I don't need to use sales pitches anymore. Use the form below, or you can print your own by going to: www.financialfreedomguarantee.com/networth.

Net Worth Calculator

Name: **As of:** [date]

Assets

Cash
Checking Accounts
Savings Accounts
CDs (Certificates of Deposit)
Life Insurance (cash surrender value)
Other Cash
Total Cash   -

Investments
Securities (stocks, bonds, mutual funds)
Treasury Bills
Other Investments
Total Investments   -

Property
Real Estate (market value)
Automobile (present value)
Bullion (silver, gold, etc)
Jewelry, Art, and Collectibles
Other Property
Total Property   -

Retirement
Retirements Accounts (CPF)
Employer Pensions
Other Assets
Total Retirement   -
Notes and Accounts Receivable

Total Assets   -

Liabilities
Accounts Payable
Auto Loan
Credit Card Debt
Consumer Loans or Installments
Loan on Life Insurance
Real Estate Mortgages
Student Loans
Unpaid Taxes
Money Owed to Others
Other Liabilities

Total Liabilities   -

Net Worth (Total Assets - Total Liabilities)   -

CHAPTER 6
BORROW!

This is a law! The science of leverage is foreign to many, yet leverage is what you have to do to create better returns that cost you less money. You will find out here that taking out the longest-term loan with the cheapest interest rate and using it to buy high-yielding assets is the way to secure your financial freedom.

This chapter is where things start to get really cool. Because it is here that I am going to show you nine ways to raise capital to get you climbing the investment property ladder. Even if you are only able to acquire a share of an asset, you will still be better off than billions of others because you will have started your first passive income stream.

When you see that money rolling into your bank account every month, you will start to believe that you can increase that wealth a lot. It will definitely happen if you follow my tried and tested blueprint.

WHY LEVERAGE IS REALLY AWESOME
It is only when you learn the power of leverage that you can truly live the charmed and bodacious life that you deserve.

It is highly unlikely that you are going to be able to buy properties with cash, that is, without needing a mortgage. And even if you did, you would run out of cash quickly. To make more money, you need to borrow money.

What billions of people do not realize is that if you buy the right property, it will go up in value. And when you borrow 80 percent to 90 percent of the original property price and then that property increases in value, the loan you originally got essentially decreases. So in two or three years your loan could have reduced to 50 percent of the property's value. And you have bucket loads of new equity that you can now *leverage*, i.e., use to buy more property. If you do this at the right time in the cycle, this process will be accelerated to its optimum degree. This is why buying at the beginning of a cycle is critical to building wealth and financial freedom quickly.

Many people reading this book are sitting on a property, or several properties, whose value they don't know. They may be sitting on cash they cannot access, because they have not leveraged the new value of the house.

I am still amazed at how many people (at least in the groups that attend my workshops) are in this situation. But when they learn my blueprint, they are financially free in literally less than three months. They usually can't believe it, but they sure thank me after, when they have quit their jobs and started doing what they love to do.

Many people with weak financial mindsets believe borrowing is risky. These people pay their house off in cash and end up with no income left for their retirement. Sadly, they die without having really lived because they spent their lives worrying about money.

If you have mastered the art of borrowing properly, you can borrow with minimal risk and create fantastic amounts of positive cash flow. Once you have replaced your salary with positive cash flow, the risk gets smaller because if you lose your job you still have an income that will allow you to live a comfortable lifestyle. This is assuming, of course, that you have purchased the right property, having done the proper research and applied the fundamentals—the main four of which I am repeating here for your benefit:

1. Buy at the beginning of a cycle.
2. Buy in suburbs where the population is growing and people have enough income to buy or rent your property.
3. Buy in towns that are constantly investing in the development of the infrastructure—things like better transportation, shopping, education, residential zoning, parks and greenery, relevant community areas, and so forth.
4. Buy in towns and cities where jobs are being created faster than the population is growing. Look for business and entrepreneurial investment. I call these *good economic factors*.

I will share in detail in the next chapter how you find that performing property to change your life. But first, as I've mentioned, you must address one core element of borrowing, and that is you must look after your credit.

POWER UP YOUR CREDIT SCORE AND GET LOANS EASILY

If the banks will not lend you money, for whatever reason you think it is, it is only comes down to one factor—your personal credit profile. This will contain your credit history with lending institutions, and all of it is on record, down to the date you make payments, all your credit cards over time, and any loans you might have, including the full balance of what you owe.

I am going to fix your credit profile here. Read this carefully and read it again and again; it may literally save your life!

Just imagine you have found that ideal property; you have sweated, you have researched, you have taken the time and made the effort. Then when you apply for the mortgage the bank declines your application. How would you feel about that?

Well folks, it's very common indeed because it's not it's not on your radar and, because once again, it was not taught in school. How is it I am still able to apply for loans and get them? I am a school dropout! I don't have a degree! I am an academic dimwit!

Yet last week, I was approved and received £2 million (about $3.1 million) in new loans to purchase two amazing apartment buildings in the United Kingdom. The great news is that this was a refinancing loan at a cheaper interest rate, which means I have more positive cash flow.

This is the art and science of borrowing; it is all about how you raise that capital. And I can tell you one more secret: I am on the lookout for new cheaper, longer-term loans every single day. Some don't work out, but some do and if you don't apply, you won't get any more money. Raising capital is a skill you can easily learn.

Before we get to my nine best ways to raise capital, let me show you how to get credit from lending institutions. Banks look at these areas, in order of priority:

1. Credit History

As soon as the bank receives your loan application, they run a credit check. In some countries, you can check on your own credit score. In the United States, you can get your credit reports free once a year from www.annualcreditreport.com. This will include reports from all three US credit bureaus. (It doesn't give you your credit scores, however; you have to pay for those. Check out www.myFICO.com.) There is nothing worse than applying for a loan, being declined, and not knowing the reason for it.

And in that credit history, the past year is what they will look at the most. If you have paid everything on time every month, month in and month out, your credit scores will be immensely stronger.

2. Debt exposure

The next step will be to see how much debt you are carrying versus what credit you have available, so if you have $100,000 of credit available, and you have balances that total $90,000 on your credit cards, etc., you only have $10,000 available.

My advice to you will eliminate this issue immediately! Pay down your debt. One way of paying down your debt is to remortgage your house and consolidate your loans into one monthly payment that you can manage more easily. A big part of creating financial freedom is how you manage your debt. The best debt to have by far is a mortgage, as the interest is less than half that of credit cards and it can be stretched over a longer period, making the payments much more affordable. Also, a good property will keep going up in value over time, while your debt will stay the same. When you know where you stand, you can move your available cash around strategically, too, and improve your credit score.

3. Income

What is your income? Is it regular and consistent? To a bank this is the most important item because if you don't have any income you cannot repay the loan. So this is the first thing you must get right. If you don't have a regular income, don't worry; you can create that income and show the banks you are financially sound. This is just an accounting juggle, but it is very easy and legal to do. I will tell you how to do this, at the end of the chapter in the "Secrets of borrowing more cash" section that follows.

4. Taxes

From a bank's point of view, you have to show you are paying taxes on a regular basis because they want to know you don't have any back taxes and are law-abiding; they want to see compliance because they will be taken to task if they are seen as not complying with the government. It kind of makes sense now, right?

Taxes require an accounting juggle. I made $10 million last year from all my business activity and only paid $35,000 in taxes—legally. When you make more money you can pay less in tax! This is why you need to be a good juggler, so keep that in mind as we move forward.

5. No Sneaky Stuff

This is where we get into the crux of what most people do not know. If the bank sees a discrepancy between your reported wages and your bank deposit statement, they will smell something fishy. Ensure that you pay your taxes and that your net salary is exactly the same as what goes into the bank.

The majority of banks will ask for bank statements going back several months to see evidence of consistency in your income. To a bank this reduces their perceived risk massively.

6. Assets (Net Worth)

It is common sense that if you have more assets you are a smaller risk to the bank. And this is true, but the reason it is at number-six on this list is because income still outshines assets in terms of getting approval for a bank loan. They want to see that you have a constant influx of cash to pay back a loan. Some people who have assets have literally no income, and subsequently will not get the loans they request. In some cases, this ends up in forced bankruptcy because they cannot maintain their current assets.

So try not to worry about having a huge net worth, as it is not the most vital factor in obtaining the right loans. The ideal situation is having assets and income, as then you can really achieve quantum growth in wealth creation. That will come if you follow my steps carefully; however, you have to start at the beginning.

7. Marital Status

Are banks religious? No. Well some maybe more than others but the only reason I list this is because to the bank a joint income is better than one income and poses less risk. Interesting, isn't it? Maybe it does pay to be married, but even if you are not, if you jointly apply with another person whose credit is equally good or better than yours, it will improve your chances of borrowing and, more critically, borrowing more. (And of course, if the person you are applying with has worse credit than you, it will bring your chances down.)

All in all, it's just common sense. People just don't think in simple terms anymore. All I have done here is decode the bank's lending criteria. By studying this chapter, you will be light years ahead of everybody else in terms of borrowing and leveraging.

One more important note: Have all the required paperwork prepared at all times, organized in a proper file. Because you will soon see that you cannot just apply to one bank, you will be applying to several banks. And you will probably do it every year, in order to refinance and get better deals. So, please ensure that you always have on hand: six months' of bank statements, two years' worth of tax returns, and all the other paperwork related to what I have mentioned above.

So, credit is given when credit is due! When you have worked at getting the necessary credit profile together, those loans will come in thick and fast, and they'll give you positive cash flow streams you never had before. How? The returns on your investments will be greater than the cost of borrowing; this is what you will learn to do in the rest of this book.

Remember, everybody starts with one property. Now I own over one hundred! And I am still applying for loans to this day. Now that I have shared with you the details of your credit profile, it is time to share with you how we raise that much needed capital for your deposits and your loans.

There are always going to be limitations set by banks and hurdles to jump over but here are the nine strategies that will help overcome all that.

TEN FINANCING STRATEGIES

1. Re-mortgage or Refinance Your Existing Property.

This strategy will only apply to people who own property. If you do not own property yet, you still need to know this strategy, because it is something you will be doing quite often in the future.

The reason you will be doing this is because your property will keep increasing in value, especially, as I repeatedly keep reminding you, when you buy the correct property with the correct fundamental research. The better you do your research, the faster your investment will appreciate. Let me quickly illustrate this.

You buy a property with this financing scenario:

$100,000 (Purchase price)

$20,000 (Deposit you paid—assuming an 80 percent mortgage; sometimes you can get 90 percent)

$80,000 (Mortgage balance)

I am keeping this very simple, as it does not have to be complicated at all. Let's imagine in three years your property increases in value by 40 percent (this is easily achievable in the right market):

$140,000 (New purchase price, if you sold)
$80,000 (Mortgage balance, or lower)

So now, when you re-mortgage, or refinance your mortgage, you can borrow up to 80 percent or 90 percent of your new property value. Of course, when you start executing this strategy, you will need to get your property officially appraised by a bank-approved appraiser. It is worth getting more than one appraisal, because they will differ. Also, keep in mind your property value will increase further if you've renovated well (more about this later).

Let's do a quick calculation:

80 percent of $140,000 is: $112,000
90 percent of $140,000 is: $126,000

Your original mortgage balance was $80,000. By executing this simple strategy, you have potentially raised another $46,000! You have raised this extra capital just by sitting on your property, and if you have purchased a performing property, you would also have been collecting great rent for the past three years. Now can you see why I love property as a vehicle to create financial freedom.

I know you have some questions right now bubbling in your head, so allow me to preempt them: "Won't my mortgage payment increase now that I have borrowed more?"

This question is most definitely coming from a conditioned part of your mind, as a lot of you will feel fear when you start thinking about taking on more debt. In previous chapters I have covered at length how critical your mindset is to your overall success.

What question would an abundant mindset ask? "How much more positive cash flow can I create now that I've borrowed more?" This is a very different question, based on focused, new thinking: thinking about returns instead of costs!

Now let's look at the costs of this refinance scenario. If we take the original mortgage of $80,000, and it is a thirty-year mortgage at, say, 4.5 percent interest. Your monthly payment will be $405.35 per month.

Now, what about the rental income you get from this property? Previously, I shared with you that I easily get at least 12 percent return (of the purchase price) on my investment properties. In this case we paid $100,000 for the property, so our rental income would be $12,000 per year or $1,000 per month. We must take some money out of that for management fees and repairs. I will be very reasonable and deduct another $100 a month out of the rent for those variable costs, so our net rental income is $900 per month.

And so:

$900 - $405.35 = $494.65 net positive cash flow per month.

Now I really do hope you are beginning to see that you can replace your salary with passive income, fire your boss, and live life on your terms. Let's take our scenario one step further so you can see how you can easily create enough cash flow to cover your living expenses and fire your boss.

If we refinance that mortgage and borrow $126,000 which is 90 percent of the increased value of $140,000, this time, the new monthly payment will be: $638.42 At first glance you can see the mortgage payment has increased. What you have not factored in yet are the potential returns you can get if you reinvest the extra $46,000 that you borrowed.

You can now use that $46,000 to create huge leverage without the need for a deposit for your next property purchase. With this new sum we can borrow more. We can also buy up to $460,000 worth of new property. You could use it to buy one property, but I would not recommend this as it is far less risky to buy multiple, cheaper, first-time buyer homes. Very often, you can get a reduced interest rate for these lesser homes.

But for our hypothetical situation, let's assume we are paying the same interest rate as before: 4.5 percent for a 30-year mortgage. So again, we are paying $638.42 on our refinanced mortgage. We use the $46,000 for (10 percent) down payments on the new houses, whose purchase prices combined total $460,000.

$460,000 - $46,000 = $414,000

So, we are now borrowing a further $414,000.

The new monthly mortgage payments for all the houses will be:

$2,097.68 + $638.42 = $2,736.10 per month

Now we look at the returns from all our investment property purchases:

(First property net rental income) $900 per month + (new properties' rental income: $460,000 x 12%) $4,600 per month – (management fees and repairs at approximately 10%) $460 per month

= $4,140 per month + $900 (from 1st property)

= (new net rental per month) $5,040

- (new mortgage payments) $2,736.10

$5,040 - $2,736.10 = $2303.90

Oh my goodness! If your salary was around $2,000 per month, in two to three years, you would have just created financial freedom for yourself! This is how mind-bogglingly powerful leverage really is.

Unfortunately most people are conditioned to leverage purchases the wrong way by buying stuff they don't need and always getting behind because what they buy does not give them a return.

You can probably take an educated guess right now as to why I always re-invest my capital. By the way, yes, I do treat myself. I have the toys, the nice clothes, watches, and cars—but remember, I only purchased them when I was financially free, never before. If I had purchased all those nice things before, I would not have had the capital to leverage my property as I have just shown you.

Before you say, "Yes, but ..." There are variables; interest can go up or down, tenants can leave your properties or a tree could fall on your house. However, when you know how to minimize risk, these events are rare and rarely unsolvable. You can always go to other banks for lower interest rates and find other tenants lining up for your rental, if you purchase the correct investment properties. And there is insurance for trees falling.

When you continually study the markets and keep up to speed on world economies, this is already a massive risk reducer. You can start to plan for events you would have never seen before and learn to spot trends.

Some people do not enjoy this; that's why I set up the Wealth Revolution Group, because I have a team of researchers who do that for me and my members. I am not asking you to join. You can also outsource your economic research very easily and cheaply.

When your finger is on the pulse, you are prepared to change markets, sell your property or refinance. It's actually a lot of fun! It's certainly a lot more fun than going to work six days a week early in the morning and coming home late at night for a job you don't really like.

And here's the news: if you do not act upon any of my strategies, that's exactly what you will be doing, and as you get older, you may end up being fired eventually and replaced by younger talent. And finally, you will continually suffer from stress, which contributes to heart disease, the number-one cause of death, worldwide.

Your heart is saying "please stop doing this work, you're killing me!" and you argue: "But I have to do it to pay the bills," and then one day your heart just gives up.

Here is a very interesting question I want you to think about very carefully:

Would you rather work for $1,480 per month (the average world salary) in a job you don't like or would you rather receive that much and more in passive income from investment property you purchased and live life on your terms, with all the time you need and no job?

To recap: with the first strategy, I have helped you purchase your first property, then multiple subsequent properties, replaced your salary, and cleared your path to financial freedom in two to three years.

For the people that already own property, and have owned it for a while—a year at least, you should be very excited, because the strategy I have just shared with you also applies to you. And if you refinance the equity in your existing property, you can be financially free in just a few months! I'm talking ninety days or less, depending how fast the bank approves your loan.

For the readers who have really concentrated on this chapter, you will start to see the importance of why you must keep your credit profile in tip-top shape and properly maintained because even if you do own property with lots of equity in it, if you can't get a loan, you are not going to be financially free.

In conversations with people I have met, I've noticed that people don't believe they are going to die. I know I am going to die and that's why I do everything now. I execute every financing strategy now because I want to enjoy the cash flow now, when I'm young, not when I'm too old to remember my name.

What is the point of having loads of cash, and leaving it in your will? Why don't you just enjoy the freedom your money can buy and help your family and those less fortunate do the same? That is what I call living. The people that don't do this, to me, they are already dead. They may be walking but they ain't living!

For the people that do not own any property and are looking to buy their first but are worried about how they are going to get that deposit together, please read the next eight strategies on raising cash. This is especially for you.

2. Sell Any Asset that is Not Performing.

What do I mean by not performing? Very simply, if the asset is not giving you any cash flow then it isn't performing. And I don't necessarily mean a property; it could be shares or stocks in the equity markets.

Sometimes you just have to know when to quit. You have to be calculating and not sentimental about these decisions. At the end of the day, if it's not giving you any cash flow now it is unlikely to ever give you cash flow.

If you have a property that is negatively geared (the mortgage payment is more than the rent) and the property is not increasing in value, so you cannot refinance it, you have to think very seriously about cutting that loose as it is turning into one hell of a liability. (In the next chapter, you will learn how to calculate if the negatively geared property you are holding is likely to turn around and perform in future years. Read carefully, because it could literally save your life. I do indeed perform CPR. It's called Critical Property Reprogramming. It's coming in chapter 7!)

If you have shares in the stock market and you are not a professional, skilled trader, and the shares are not increasing in value or giving you any kind of cash flow you have to think seriously about selling those shares.

I have met so many people whose shares keep decreasing in value yet they hold onto them with the false hope that they will return to the "good old days." I can tell you that none of those people have enjoyed good fortune and when they finally realize they are chasing fresh air, most of them liquidate their position in the market!

3. Cash Out.

Use any fixed deposit/savings account or share holdings to purchase below-market-value investment properties. Keep an emergency fund, however, equal to between three and six months of your salary. Surrender all life insurance policies that have an investment plan built into them; these give terrible returns if any, and you are paying the sales commissions of the life insurance agents and providing the insurance company profits. (And they use these profits to buy the tallest buildings in most cities, to show everyone they are financially stable and trustworthy!) You are better just getting term life and medical insurance, without any investment element. It's far cheaper.

Cash out shares in "protect profit cycles," meaning if you have stock that has made a profit, get out of the market (unless you are an experienced trader, making good money at it).

First things first: always minimize your risk. The very first risk reducer, mentioned above, is a solid emergency cash fund that you can always access.

Why? While you are on your journey to financial freedom and building your new passive income streams, things you did not plan for can suddenly hit. For example, you could lose your job and if you do not yet have enough passive income from your rents to live on, you still need to pay your bills. An emergency fund is essential for any other eventuality, too, such as unexpected sickness, accidents, and so forth.

If you have no cash and no one to borrow from, you could easily end up in bankruptcy and when that happens, you won't be able to get credit or borrow any money for at least six years. Please do not get yourself into that position.

How do you get your hands on more cash? I'm going to go old-school here and suggest you get more than one job temporarily to save up some cash. This also applies for your first property deposit. Good old hard work and financial sacrifice is necessary on occasion. You will be glad you did it, and you can actually enjoy it when, and only when, you know the money you are making has the distinct purpose of making you financially free. You will be amazed how much energy you have when you undertake all this part-time work. Do anything! Clean windows, mop floors—it doesn't matter. Wouldn't you rather work your ass off for the next six months to two years than work your ass off for the rest of your life? Freedom or slavery—it's your choice. I chose to work my ass off and eventually it paid off.

In summary: sell what does not or is not likely to give you a return, get the cash.

4. Obtain a Bridge Loan.

Sometimes you have no choice other than to obtain an unsecured loan to bridge a buy. This can be through a credit card, a personal loan, or an official bridge loan.

Have I ever used this option? Yes. Do I still use this option? Yes. When you are purchasing at below-market value, auction, or bankrupt developer property, you have to act very, very quickly or run the risk that one of your competitors will snap it up.

When a fantastic property comes along at a very cheap price it is never on the market for long because smart investors and entrepreneurs will go for it like rabid dogs.

Your job is to learn how to source those investments for yourself. But be prepared, because if you source it and you cannot get the finances in time you are going to lose out and cry for months. Most private auctions only give you thirty days to complete the payment.

I do not ever have to worry about this because through my own network, I already have bridge loan finance available to me. And, because I always service my loans I get approved within forty-eight hours. Arguably, the interest rates are high. On some deals I pay 0.99 percent per month or just under 12 percent per year. However, the longest I have held a property on this type of loan is six months. By this time I would have refinanced the entire deal and switched to paying around 4 percent to 5 percent interest instead.

What's awesome about this is that because I got the deal under value to begin with, I end up with loads more cash. Here's how this strategy works.

Property appraised at: $1,680,000

Purchase price: $860,000

Deposit: $172,000 (raised either through crowd-funding or profit from my own investment properties)

Balance (80%): $688,000

Mortgage payment: $7,076.85 per month

Rental collection per month: $10,800

Refinance after six months

New appraisal: $1,950,000

Refinance balance (70%): $1,365,000

Terms: 30-year, 4.5%

New Mortgage Payment: $6,916.25

Cash in my pocket: $677,000

No, your eyes are not deceiving you. This is a real deal I did in the last six months and I just had the refinance approved. I still collect

$3,883.75 in rent every single month. And a whopping $677,000 in my bank account that I can reinvest—out of one deal.

Yes, it did take me a while to get to these deals, as we did the hard work first. And remember this: I paid the deposit for my first ever house on my credit card which is also a bridge loan.

5. Purge.

Sell everything that you have not used for at least six months in a garage sale, to friends, or on Craigslist or eBay. EBay has been a revelation in giving your unused stuff a new life and of course giving you some cash as reward. (This strategy can raise a deposit.)

I remember seeing some expert on the *Oprah Winfrey Show*, saying that if you have not used something in six months you are very unlikely to ever use it again. Don't be a hoarder. Check your attic, cellar, spare room, closets and drawers—you will be shocked at how much stuff you have. Sell it!

Indeed if you have ever moved recently, you probably noticed you've been packing and unpacking "stuff" that you never use. And you will just keep moving to bigger houses so you can keep storing it all.

Some of you reading this book will be astonished to find that you can actually raise a property deposit by doing this. Indeed it could set you on your journey to financial freedom.

6. Seller Finance

In desperate times, sellers are sometimes willing to split the deposit or whole cost of a property, over several monthly installments, that make it possible for you to afford it! You must understand the value of desperate sellers.

A desperate seller is one that cannot sell their property at the price that they desire, but they urgently need the money. The longer the property sits unsold, the more desperate they become. I call these scenarios the three Ds: debt, divorce, and death.

They are the three major reasons desperate sellers are selling. Debt is the most common circumstance, followed closely by a disposing of assets because a couple is getting divorced, and last, disposing of belongings after a relative's death.

Once you have found this particular kind of seller, you have met your most profitable opportunity, simply because of how fast they need the money. Once you dangle a bit of cash in front of their eyes, even though it is far below their asking price, you will attract their attention because they so desperately want any cash they can get hold of.

In a nutshell you have two profit centers in one deal:

a. Below-market value property. The more desperate the seller, the more discount you will get off the purchase price of a property. (And please note, the best property investors make the most profit when they buy the property not when they sell it.)

b. The next profit center is how far you can spread your payments, while locking in the purchase price. This is really how long you can defer paying the whole amount of the deposit, as in all of my property purchases I never, ever pay all the deposit up front. I always negotiate time to pay, and this helps your cash flow considerably!

Now, I have not yet really explained seller finance, also called *vendor finance*, and this is very sexy. Here goes. Imagine there is a property for sale from a desperate seller.

Sale price: $150,000
Appraisal: $200,000

The first benefit you should see here is that this property is 25 percent below market value and therein is your first profit center. If, of course you have done your research (more on this in the next chapter), you have locked in $50,000 in profit from day one.

Mortgage (80%): $120,000

This would mean you would have to find $30,000 deposit to complete the deal. You might already have this cash or you might not. Even if you do have it, it's always better to let your cash work a little harder for you.

You can offer the seller $150,000, on condition that the seller finances your deposit over six or twelve monthly installments. If you can get that seller to let you pay the deposit in twelve installments…that's only $2,500 per month.

You can also negotiate with the seller to let you place a tenant in the property and collect rent throughout the twelve-month period, even though you don't own the property yet.

If the rent is, say, $1,200, that means you are now only paying $1,300 per month over twelve months, interest-free, for the deposit on the property. In one year that property will most certainly increase in value, so actually you have three profit centers in one deal now.

c.   This profit center is a one-year freeze on your purchase price.

If the property increases by 15 percent, (which it will if you follow my "precise research analysis" methods in the next chapter), that will mean you will lock in another $30,000 in profit on the same property. Confused? Let's look at it again:

Appraisal: $200,000
Value increase: 15%

New appraisal: $230,000

In summary, you have now locked in $80,000 in profit within one year with only a $15,600 investment.

The return on this deal will astound you:

$80,000 x 100% = 512% return on $15,600

I will explain this calculation for you because I know right now you are reeling from disbelief and shock. But you can probably now see why I love property and the opportunities it gives me!

We have agreed to a deal with a $150,000 purchase price, requiring a $30,000 deposit. The seller has agreed to allow us to finance the deposit over twelve months and allowed us to put in our tenant. This means our installment is $2,500 per month for twelve months. However, because we have placed a tenant in the property paying $1,200 per month, our net payment for this property per month is $1,300.

There is no mortgage payment yet because the seller has agreed to complete this deal one year from now. The 512 percent return is how much profit we have made after one year, assuming the property has gained 15 percent in that time. Remember also, we have already locked in $50,000 profit because the property is being purchased at 25 percent below the market price.

Is this sexy? You're damn right it is and yet there is also another opportunity to make money within that same twelve months. Brace yourselves.

You can flip this property to another buyer within that twelve-month period and keep all the profit you make! You can even do a longer deal with the seller over five to ten years. This is called *lease with the option to purchase.*

Let's all cool down so I can summarize: you can easily sell the property you do not own to another buyer. For example, at $180,000, you will make an instant profit of $30,000. But now, how do you freeze the price of a property over five years with a desperate seller?

You can do this by simply offering to pay the seller's mortgage for them and agreeing to a small up-front sweetener fee, of between 2 percent and 5 percent of the property's value.

So if the property value is $200,000 you can offer up to $10,000 cash up front, and offer to pay their mortgage for them, or even a little more, because when you agree to this deal, you can put your own tenant in, and collect all the rent, because you now control this property for the full five years.

By doing this, you can create positive cash flow from the income from the tenant. Is it legal? This is probably the most common question I get asked at this stage. Yes, it is legal and a lease-option purchase agreement can be prepared by qualified lawyers to protect you and the seller.

The seller cannot back out of the agreement. They have the obligation to freeze the price for you for an agreed time. You, on the other hand, have the option to exit the deal at any time.

You would probably agree with me by now that this is a fantastic strategy, and you would be correct. I have done a lot of deals in my time in this way. When you don't have much capital you are forced to be more creative and explore other ways.

7. Share a Purchase.

It is better to have 25 percent of something than 100 percent of nothing. If you cannot use the previous six strategies, this is a must option. Today's world is all about how good a communicator you are and connecting with more people, especially online. Why don't you start using your existing connections to help you fund your next property purchase?

When you're starting out it is very challenging to raise a deposit for your first house because in this climate especially first-time buyers cannot borrow enough money from the bank, as their salaries aren't enough. For example, in Sydney, Australia, you would have to travel three hours outside of the city to afford your first house. This is the same with London and New York.

But by using your online network you can now very easily Crowd-fund a property purchase by sharing the cost of the deposit and mortgage, and still achieve the same returns on your money. This means your money is working better for you because you are leveraging the purchase with others. Again, a qualified lawyer can draft a simple shareholders agreement to protect all the buyers of the house so it is entirely fair. There are even Crowd-fund companies, like the one I have developed, that will find the other shareholders for you.

Let's take an example: You find a house for $100,000. You can get an 80% mortgage so, $80,000, is covered by the bank. That leaves you needing to source $20,000 plus other buyer's costs. If there are four of you buying the property, you will only have to use $5,000 of your own money, which you could even put on a credit card. With this strategy you are on the property ladder and your property is making positive cash flow and giving you a great return on your money. Given that you buy the right property your cash can start doing this for you:

Mortgage: $80,000 (at 2.99% with a 30-year term)
Monthly payment: $332.98
Rental (assuming 12%): $1,000 per month
Net cash in your pocket: $667.02
Divided by four shareholders: $166.75 each per month

That means you are making $2,001.06 per year from a $5,000 investment, a magnificent 40 percent return. It really is possible but the sad thing is hardly anyone knows how to do this because they have not been taught how.

And it does not stop there. I didn't include the increase in value of the property year after year. If we again assume a 15 percent increase in value after the first year, we have $15,000 of new profit between four shareholders, amounting to $3,750 each. If we add that on to the return we get from our original $5,000 investment that is a new combined return of 115 percent.

Let me just stop you here and ask: are you getting between 40 percent and 115 percent return from the $5,000 currently in your bank account?

You know the answer to that, but just to illustrate my point of how much a bank is ripping you off: an average savings account worldwide offers 1 percent per year before tax. That is a ridiculous measly figure of $50 a year. What the hell is anyone doing that for!

If you can't raise a deposit on your own, share the purchase, and start smiling.

8. Become a Trustee.

No money, no honey—but there is always a way. Consider being a trustee for an investor and take a share of the property. Investors need trustees to extend mortgages and credit. There are certain situations where this strategy can come in very handy.

Imagine you cannot borrow any more money from the bank; you are at your limit, your credit has run out . What if you could put the mortgage under someone else's name yet still control the property and enjoy the benefits of full ownership in terms of cash flow and capital gain? With a trustee/beneficiary agreement you can do exactly this.

This is how it works. You find someone—maybe one of your children, a friend, or a relative—and you offer them a share of the property without them having to put in any cash. All they do is take the loan in their name so you can gain the advantage of a 30-year mortgage with a lower payment.

You pay the deposit and offer the trustee (the person who is taking the mortgage under their name) a percentage of the cash flow the property generates and the capital gain the property accumulates. Normally I offer 25 percent of the entire deal.

So if the rent is $1,000 per month, the trustee would receive $250 a month, pretty much for doing nothing. They would also get a 25 percent share of the property's value. So when the property sold, for example, at a profit of $100,000, the trustee would receive $25,000.

In a trustee arrangement such as this, there are two documents:

1. The trustee/beneficiary agreement, which stipulates how much you are both entitled to; and
2. The power of attorney, which the trustee signs to give you, the beneficiary, full control over the property so that the trustee cannot sell the property without your say so.

They are both very important documents; however, the power of attorney is the most important as it gives you legal control of the property. Without this document the agreement is useless and too risky. A qualified lawyer can draft this agreement for you.

9. Use your PENSION (IRA/401K) to Invest in Property!!!!

I am to this day dumbfounded that the American Public in general has no idea they can do this...so let's get this straight...

All retirement accounts in the US are "self directed". Investors don't realize this.... they think they need to use big firms like Merrill Lynch... T Rowe Price... Fidelity.... all of these companies are CUSTODIANS for the money who also INVEST the money. These companies take millions of management fees out and give you a pathetic 3 to 4% on average paid back into your Pension.

In the USA, your 401k/IRA can purchase and be the owner of Properties!!! The property then returns all the Cash-flow back into your IRA…This means instead of the literally stupid returns of 3%, you can get between 10 and 25% per annum on average. This is one of the ultimate no-brainer decisions you will ever make in your life!

10. Create Companies.

A company can pay you a new salary and thereby extend your credit! I would say this is one of the coolest and most effective strategies I have ever used.

I have stated earlier in this book that rich people own companies and poor people work for companies. This is the only strategy where on paper you can be both rich and poor, yet in reality become a lot richer! There will be times when you simply run out of credit, and the bank will tell you that you cannot borrow any more money because your income is too low and you have reached your limit.

You see, all banks have a formula for how much you can borrow. Generally, this formula says that you can only borrow three to four times your annual salary. So if you earn $100,000 per year, you will only be able to borrow $400,000 maximum.

When you have purchased the house, and even when the property increases in value, you will only be able to borrow the maximum of $400,000, which limits any more property purchases. As I mentioned earlier, the most important detail to a bank when you apply for a loan is your credit profile and monthly income.

If you can somehow increase your monthly income, you can borrow more. With this in mind, my students and I have used this unique strategy to successfully borrow a hell of a lot more money than we normally could have.

CHAPTER 7

MASTER PRECISE RESEARCH ANALYSIS (PRA)

I n this chapter I will show you how to research property investments—and how to analyze your research—what to look for and how to sustain investment performance for the long term. This chapter contains two extremely valuable guides. First is my exhaustive Financial Freedom Buyer's Guide, with how-to's on everything from how to choose the right property and finance it to how to choose the right tenant and the details of a solid rental agreement. Second is the Four Fundamentals Due Diligence Checklist, a concise reference with all the resources you need to thoroughly research each of the Four Ultimate Fundamentals of Property Investing that I taught you in chapter 3.

This is where I save your life. This is where I perform CPR, a.k.a., Critical Property Reprogramming. This is where I change the way that you (and most people) think about property. Instead of buying something that looks nice, you will buy something that gives you sustained returns, the golden ticket of living a life of freedom instead of a life of constant servitude to salary that is never enough.

I invite you to reread chapter 3 and refresh your memory of my Four Ultimate Fundamentals of Property Investing before I go into detail on the necessary, full due diligence required for investing in your next property. Every piece of relevant research you do reduces your risk of losing money.

WHY IT'S A GREAT TIME TO BE A LANDLORD

For most of you, the money you have made over the years is from a salary. Because it has come from a salary, it would have taken you years to save up for a decent property to buy. Unfortunately the gap between salary and property affordability has widened a great deal, resulting in very few first-time buyers being able to get on the property ladder.

Since the global financial crisis, banks have significantly tightened their lending policies, and now a majority of approved loans require a 20 percent deposit, which is out of reach for most working class people. However, this is great news for landlords, as the rental market has gone crazy. The big deposits have scared away the potential first-time buyers, creating the opportunity for those people to become renters and your tenants.

When you have fully studied this book, you will have the know-how to be a landlord and create great income streams from those tenants— income streams that create financial freedom for you!

THE FINANCIAL FREEDOM BUYER'S GUIDE

I am going to put this guide entire book online for you, so you can easily access this reference anywhere at any time. The link is www. financialfreedomguarantee/buyersguide. But here, I will summarize everything you need to know about property investing in fourteen points. It's a concise buyer's guide for you to refer back to.

1. Choose Income Property (VS. Capital Gain Property)

Income property is the term for a house whose monthly mortgage payment is less than what is collected in rent. Capital gain property describes real estate you would buy looking toward future, potential profits rather than immediate cash flow. Here's the rule, folks: if you are not financially free, meaning you still have to work, the last thing you should be buying is capital gain property that has no positive cash flow or is negatively geared (the mortgage payment is higher than what you receive in rent). Why? Very simply, what would happen if you lost your job or for some reason you could not work? How are you going to pay that mortgage?

Buying capital gain property is extremely risky when you still have to work. My advice is to not go anywhere near that kind of property until you are financially free! When you have replaced your salary with passive income from your assets, this is when you can consider buying property that comes with potential, rather than existing, income.

Holding capital gain property with zero or negative income could be the fastest route to bankruptcy. You will lose your credit and get "blacklisted" and be unable to borrow for at least five years in most countries! You would miss an entire cycle of opportunity, which could cost you dearly—so dearly that you would have to work until you die!

2. The Magic of BMV (Below Market Value)

If you remember what I stated earlier, you make most of your profit when you buy a property, not when you sell it. So in your calculations (which I will show you later) you must factor in how much below the true market value your targeted property is. As a guideline, I like to be at least 20 percent below the market price. So if the market value of a property is $100,000 you should be getting it for $80,000.

People who are not focused on investing may get blinded by emotion—e.g., how beautiful a property is. These people will not see the price as priority. They will only see "how nice it looks"…

No matter how lovely the stonework on the garage, the cabinets and design of the kitchen, the beautiful floors—if you are not able to get anywhere near 20 percent below market value, you have to walk away. This is because it's going to be so much harder trying to make profit later, when you're trying to sell.

One note on market value: you can gain a lot of insight by looking at the listings on big property websites in the area such as Realtor.com and Zillow.com. However, what they list is not necessarily the true market value. Some list enticing deals just to get you to inquire and then tell you the property is no longer available, but that they do have one even better that is slightly more expensive but definitely worth a look! This is a very common strategy by real estate agents to get your name and e-mail address so they can keep targeting you. Be very careful and smart!

3. Location

Now we come to what you may think is the simplest factor: where the property is located. When you do the proper research (I'll outline later), this will become really easy to narrow down. On this critical feature, you are limited by your budget and what you can borrow. For example, if you were targeting the United Kingdom for your first investment property purchase, you would find that London is not going to give you any positive cash flow situations, simply because the property there is too expensive. New York and California offer similar restrictions.

You can target locations outside of London where your return could be at least 7 percent. You can use 7 percent minimum as a guideline, in fact, but you should really be looking at 8 percent to 10 percent annual returns. These returns don't include any increase in value the property has, because I am targeting cash flow and income to replace your salary first. This will focus your target to specific areas that can offer that yield, subject to the Four Ultimate Fundamentals of Property Investing firing on all cylinders! (See page 120 for the Four Fundamentals Due Diligence Checklist and the research tools that will tell you.)

4. Tenant Profiling

Once you've found a property to target, the next question to ask is whether or not the place is tenanted. Let me ask you another question: if the property you are targeting is already tenanted, is that going to reduce your risk or increase it?

Think about that for a moment, as most property buyers completely disregard this information, thinking that's just a small thing. Most people think they can get a tenant, no problem. Ladies and gentlemen, I know people who have been trying to rent their properties for five years and longer. Can you imagine paying that mortgage every month while you are still waiting for a tenant to occupy? Yes, heart attack territory!

One of my golden rules is: always ensure your property is tenanted before you buy. If you find an excellent property and for whatever reason there is no tenant you must find a tenant. Simply get an agent to find a tenant for you, or advertise yourself. It is definitely worth the small expense. If you are smart it won't cost you anything at all—just ask the local real estate agents to find one for you.

In some cases you can get a spare key from the owner if you say you need to show friends and family. If you're smart, you will just ask for multiple viewings (which is very common) and take the prospective tenant with you. Hard to believe? Believe it, this is how serious investors play the game and reduce their risk of buying substantially.

If you still cannot find a tenant then there is most definitely a big hole in your research. Perhaps there are not enough jobs in the area or there is an environmental or transportation problem in that area. Or there was a famous murder in that house, which, by the way, puts a lot of people off as you can imagine.

All you are doing in each step of this guide is minimizing your risk and maximizing your opportunity. My advice is to treat every step very seriously and do not skip anything. I have seen so many disasters happen when people take shortcuts. Due diligence was invented for good reason.

5. Tenant Agreement Checklist

Of course you are going to need a sound and legal rental agreement to protect you. The agreement has to be good—so good it is going to pre-qualify your tenant, in order to prevent as many eventualities as possible, including one of the worst outcomes, eviction! Check the local landlord-tenant laws where you're buying; they can vary widely from place to place.

There is no such thing as a perfect tenant or perfect agreement. However you can get pretty close, so if anything unfortunate does happen, you can use the law effectively to get another tenant in as seamlessly as possible.

The first and most important step once you have a possible tenant is to get as much financial information about them as possible, because when they have money in their bank account, your risk of not getting paid is minimized significantly.

Here's your tenant checklist (again, laws vary and may dictate things like deposits and information you can request, etc.):

- ✓ **Three months' worth of pay stubs.**
- ✓ **Three months' worth of bank statements showing paycheck deposits.** Also, make sure they have enough money to cover three months' worth of rent in case of emergency.
- ✓ **Online credit check.** To make sure they have a good history of paying things on time.

✓ **Previous employer's reference and phone number.** Call them to see if you can find out if they have been a good boy or girl, before you invite them to live in your home! Note: The employer may not release any information like this, but you can ask.

✓ **Existing employer's contact info.** Call to verify employment.

✓ **Get a guarantor for the tenant if they have been in employment for less than one year!** The guarantor is the person who has to pay the rent if the tenant cannot, so it's an important step to take. Guarantors will still have to provide the same paperwork as the tenant, including proof of their funds and pay stubs for at least three months.

✓ **Collect a deposit.** Ensure the deposit is competitive to the area's rental market, meaning it's similar to other rental deposits in the area and not prohibitive to tenants. This could be equivalent to one month's rent.

✓ **Never, ever give keys to the tenant until the deposit check has cleared.**

✓ **Security deposit.** In case of damage to the property that you discover after the tenant moves out. Again, find out what's standard in the area.

✓ **Know your eviction law details.** Causes for eviction must be stipulated in the agreement very clearly and it must state that it follows the law of the country/state where the property is located. Please note in the United States, each state has different laws. If you do not follow these laws the tenant has the right to sue you and stay in your house without paying rent. This happens more than you could ever imagine (hence the reason I am taking the time to list all this out for you!). It is very comforting to know, when you own property in the US city of Indianapolis, that if the tenant misses one month's payment, essentially they have thirty days to make good or they will be evicted. And I don't mean you send them a letter and ask them to leave; the local sheriff will visit the property with your local property agent and physically remove them. I like that!

✓ **Inventory your entire property's contents.** List everything, down to how many knives and forks (if furnished), the brand and model of the washing machine, the lint basket in the clothes dryer—everything. Put a realistic replacement value on each item. Please ensure you or your agent treats this part of the agreement as a declaration, which you both sign. (Meaning, the tenants confirm that everything on the list is in fact there at the time they occupy, so if anything goes missing the tenant is liable to pay.)

✓ **An on-time payment discount.** To encourage your tenant to pay early or on time every month, offer a small cash incentive. This can be as little as $25. The property agreements I have in place all have this clause. Why? Because it works and helps you manage your money more efficiently.

✓ **A late-payment penalty.** For example, if a tenant's payment is more than seven days late, you can charge them a fee or interest. (If there is a direct debit in place this should never happen).

✓ Ensure monthly rent will be paid through direct debit from the tenant's bank. This must be signed at the onset, when they are signing the rental agreement, and there must be proof from the bank that it's been set up before they move in.

This checklist is very comprehensive and covers all aspects of risk. I am not going to include a full rental agreement because these are readily available online and your property manager or rental agent will have their preferred templates. Your job is to inspect that agreement and insert the above clauses if they are not included. Also get it checked out by a local lawyer who specializes in property.

And on that same note, you need to find a good rental/property management agent before you even think about renting out your new property. Start with the local property managers in the area, and do your due diligence on these agents; ensure that they have staff, an office, and plenty of tenants on their books. You can also check them out on the Internet in online forums. Agents' names will be flagged if they're bad. Your agreement with your rental agent should be for a maximum of one year, with an escape clause of thirty days if they do not perform to the specified requirements of your contract. This might be: not collecting rents on time, not attending to damage or maintenance, or not keeping you fully informed of a change in tenant, etc.

I'm telling you all this because there are many bad property managers out there. The most popular con that property managers will use is telling you the house needs a repair when it doesn't and sending you a fake bill. You are especially vulnerable to this if you live in a different country, which is often the case for me.

To prevent such fraud, your vetting process must be good, and your agreement must protect you. There are also landlord associations that will help protect you. The best property managers I have found are through referrals from my personal friends.

6. Calculate Yield and Income (or Loss).

You have to do the numbers as soon as you have identified a potentially great property. The numbers have to stack up, guys.

I am going to show you an example of a typical property scenario in 2015 as I write this book. I am not going to tell you the country it's from yet; let's see if you can guess.

Average house price: $810,000
Average rent $2,360 per month
Average yield 3.5% (gross)

10% deposit: $81,000

Monthly, 30-year mortgage at 4.5%=$3,597.47 per month

Positive cash flow? No, you'd be losing $1,237.47 per month, not including maintenance costs. Would a property like this give you financial freedom? No. This Property is what we call *negatively geared*. The rent does not cover the mortgage payment. In fact, it's the worst kind of investment property you can buy when you are not financially free. It means you will have to find an extra $1,237.47 per month just to be able to hold onto the property to try and enjoy any capital gain.

Unfortunately with this particular scenario above, in that particular country, it is more likely property will drop in price before it gains. Why? You are at the very top of a cycle. The next part of the cycle in this country is a correction sideways and downwards.

The country is Australia, and the city is Perth. So those dollars were actually Australian.

Now the above is based on house averages, so what we could do is go the apartment route, or what they call it in Australia, a *unit*. Let's have a look:

Average unit price in Perth: A$491,600 (about $351,000)

Average rent: A$2,000 per month

Average yield 4.8% (gross)

10% deposit: A$49,160

Monthly, 30-year mortgage at 4.5%=A$2,241.47

Positive cash flow? No, you'd be losing A241.47 per month, not including maintenance costs. The average capital gain on property in Perth for 2014 was 1.2 percent. This will not bring you financial freedom. The yield for the rent is 4.8 percent, much better, but we are still negatively geared.

Also, maintenance costs in apartments are higher because of the services they provide. Typically, there will be a monthly service charge or management fees. This can easily touch 5 percent to 10 percent of the rent, even more in some apartment blocks and countries. Depending on who pays these fees, your minus-$A241 could quickly turn into minus-A$500.

When you follow my blueprint, these properties are easy to spot and say: "These are not my target properties!" When you hear yourself say something like this, it's the moment of truth. The moment when you know your search for positive-cash-flow investments truly begins. You should feel good about yourself knowing that you are not going to encumber yourself with more debt. You have saved yourself from possible financial ruin.

Unfortunately most people buy properties like "lemmings," they buy what everybody is buying. The government's encouragement may make you even feel patriotic about buying your own home. You might feel more homey and attached and secure, when in fact you've bought the wrong home at the wrong price and have gotten yourself into more stress and worry for years to come.

Now let's look at a flat (apartment) in London:

Average flat price: £600,000 (about $922,000)
Average rent: £2,000 per month
Average yield: 4% (gross)
10% Deposit: £60,000
Mortgage, 25-year term, at 3.99% = £2,847 per month

Positive cash flow? No, you'd be losing £847 per month (about $1,300), not including maintenance costs. Capital gain the previous year? 1 percent. No, that's still not working, you are still a slave! No chance of early retirement here!

Ok, it's time to check out the main cities in the United States. Let's try New York and Los Angeles:

Average house price: $600,000
Average rent: $2,000 per month
Average yield 3.5% (gross)
10% Deposit: $60,000
Mortgage, 30-year term, at 4.5% = $2,847 per month

Positive cash flow? No, you'd be losing $847 per month! And about that capital gain the year before: 0 percent.

I can tell you these sorry numbers are similar in Asian countries, too, like Singapore, China, and Malaysia. It's because they are all at the top of a high cycle that is already correcting sideways and downwards. There are just no first-time-buyer homes in these places, and it's first-time buyers who dictate the cycles in every property market around the world. We now call these people "Generation Renters," because they cannot afford a deposit on a house.

If you want to do the calculations to find out the average yield and income from investing in property in your own area, you can find everything you need to do so at the end of this chapter. You will discover simple ways to calculate all the data you need to make a proper informed decision.

7. Monthly Income From Rent You Must Achieve.

To make it super simple, all you have to do is focus on two numbers:

1. Monthly mortgage payment
2. Monthly rent collected

It really is simple. You have to decrease the mortgage payment as much as possible and you have to increase the rent as much as possible. And if you have been reading, absorbing, and learning from this book, you have probably figured out that the easiest way to do that is to invest in low-cost, first-time-buyer homes. Those homes, however, also have to meet the criteria of the Four Ultimate Fundamentals of Property Investing (cycles, demographics, development structure, local and global economies, including job growth).

These investments, take less capital and give higher returns. Of course there are exceptions, like the Australia mining towns situation; however, those homes were unique in that they were the first houses ever built there.

Now let's take Manchester as an example:

Property price: £80,000 (about $123,000)

Rent: £600 per month

Rental yield: 9% (gross)

5% deposit (for UK citizens who are qualified first-time buyers*): £4,000

Mortgage, 30-year term, at 2.99%: £300 per month.

Monthly service charge average: £20 per month

Total Costs: £320

*10% to 30% for unqualified buyers or foreigners (remember, crowd-fund deposit possible!)

Positive cash flow? Yes! £280 per month! And just to sweeten it further, the property had a capital gain the previous year of 15 percent. As Austin Powers so eloquently said, "Yeah baby!"

Well, here we have a very different investment, giving you fantastic positive cash flow immediately. If we calculate your net salary at £2,000 per month you can see you would only need to buy approximately six of these properties to achieve financial freedom!

My question now to you is this: How could you buy fewer properties and achieve the same net income per month?

Some of you may have already worked it out; there are really only two ways (assuming, always, that your Fundamentals criteria have been met).

Decrease the monthly mortgage payment.
Increase the monthly rental income.

You can decrease the mortgage payment by either getting the bank to lower your interest rate, taking an interest-only mortgage or taking a longer-term mortgage. You will definitely have to approach different banks and shop around for the best interest rate and lowest payment.

If we apply, for example, the "taking a longer-term mortgage" strategy to the Manchester example, you can see how your positive cash flow increases substantially!

Property price: £80,000
Rent: £600 per month
Rental yield: 9% (gross)
5% deposit (for UK citizens who are qualified first-time buyers*): £4,000
Mortgage, 35-year term, at 2.99%: £180 per month.
Monthly service charge average: £20 per month
Total Costs: £200

New positive cash flow? £400 per month! Now you only need five properties to be financially free! Before you assume that it is not possible to extend mortgage terms and lower interest rates, you are utterly mistaken. You can even reduce the interest rate with your own bank today by just picking up the phone and telling them you are going to shift your mortgage to another bank because they are too expensive and other banks offer cheaper rates (which they do).

Your bank will likely offer you a better rate. They do not ever want to lose a great customer, as they know acquiring new customers is very competitive, and they also know you will probably subscribe to their other products, including credit cards, etc. It is in their interest to reduce your rate, as it is a small cost to keep you.

So call them today! You will be very surprised what you can get and more importantly how much more cash flow you can generate. I advise my students to do this on the first day I meet them.

8. Historical Capital Appreciation

To get a much clearer picture of how a potential property will perform in the future, we must first reach into the past. This is an interesting subject because when you see how the property has gained or lost value over time, it can set off an avalanche of information that will empower you to make a far better investment decision.

You can cross check your research on the four fundamentals (cycles, demographics, development plan, job growth) to see if any of those affected the gains or losses on the property in question. For example, if a new company came to town and employed hundreds of new people, did the property's price and/or rent increase subsequently? If there was a new train station built (development plan) did more people move to the area (population growth). Did banks lower mortgage interest rates and minimum deposits (things that majorly influence the cycle)?

You can get more detailed information—in some cases, for the specific property you're looking at—from the land registry offices where all sales are recorded. Here are links to some of those.

United Kingdom: https://www.gov.uk/search-property-
information-land-registry

Australia: http://www.australia.gov.au/content/land-
titles

United States: https://www.uslandrecords.com/uslr/
UslrApp/index.jsp

UK House Price Index

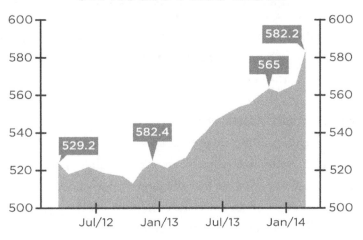

Source: http://www.ons.gov.uk/ons/taxonomy/index.html?nscl=House+Price+Indices

As you can see, there has been a rapid recovery in the UK market since 2012. Before that, prices were coming down and the United Kingdom was still in a slump cycle.

Ratio between house prices and income

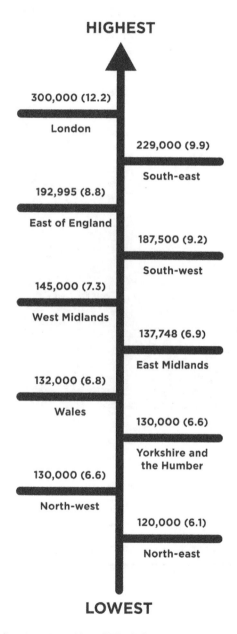

HIGHEST

300,000 (12.2)
London

229,000 (9.9)
South-east

192,995 (8.8)
East of England

187,500 (9.2)
South-west

145,000 (7.3)
West Midlands

137,748 (6.9)
East Midlands

132,000 (6.8)
Wales

130,000 (6.6)
Yorkshire and the Humber

130,000 (6.6)
North-west

120,000 (6.1)
North-east

LOWEST

Source: http://www.theguardian.com/uk-news/2015/sep/02/housing-market-gulf-salaries-house-prices

This graph also includes London, which has heavily influenced the overall rise, as it has outperformed every other city. (However, Manchester is now beating London in terms of capital growth.)

Singapore House Price Index

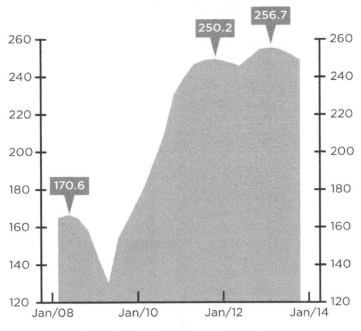

Source: https://www.ura.gov.sg/uol/property-market.aspx

Here is Singapore. Notice the extreme rise in property prices after the financial crisis in 2008. In Singapore, I tripled my money in three years in select districts. Today is a very different picture; now, property is decreasing in value through a new slump cycle.

The United States is a different picture completely.

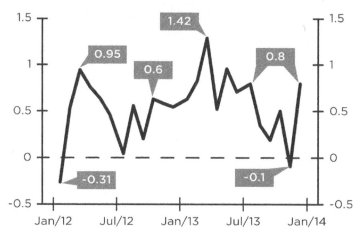

United States House Price Index MOM Change

Source: http://www.fhfa.gov/DataTools/Downloads/pages/house-price-index.aspx

Please note, the USA is a very different country in many ways. It is set up into 50 states with each state having its own economy and government. And there is a massive disparity in the states where my properties are managed. For example, Detroit, Michigan is a bankrupt city with massive financial problems. Texas is the richest state and has low taxes overall and no income tax.

You will find that new markets appeared in the United States, as discussed earlier, such as Indianapolis, because of huge job losses and wage cuts. People simply moved to cheaper states and consequently the property values in those states increased as the population migrated.

Cost of buying a home in different cities

Atlanta: $35,800

Baltimore: $52,662

Boston: $80,050

Chicago: $54,346

Cleveland: $32,010

Cincinnati: $33,485

Dallas: $48,787

Denver: $61,642

Detroit: $35,521

Houston: $49,983

Los Angeles: $89,665

Miami: $58,431

Minneapolis: $47,627

New York: $87,536

Orlando: $42,143

Philadelphia: $50,914

Pittsburgh: $31,716

Phoenix: $40,658

Portland: $60,603

Sacramento: $58,412

San Antonio: $45,374

San Diego: $95,433

San Francisco: $142,448

Seattle: $72,844

St. Louis: $33,323

Tampa: $37,732

Washington: $77,395

Source: http://nmhc.org/Content.aspx?id=4708

9. Type of Property

This is an area people make huge mistakes in—chasing what they think to be big profits. Different types of property will have different kinds of tenants with different kinds of risks. Let's look at some of the kinds of property available (these are the four categories I invest in):

<u>Residential</u>
Apartments
Houses
Condominiums
Student accommodations
<u>Business</u>
Offices
Retail
Hotel/motel
<u>Land</u>
Agricultural
Land Banking
Land Planning
<u>Crowd-funding</u>

Residential

I mainly invest in residential property, as you have probably gathered while reading this book. Of course the first-time-buyer homes are the lowest risk and will give the highest return if again you stick to the four fundamentals and do your due diligence.

When you start researching, you will discover that each town/city you are considering buying in will have a different set of circumstances. The first question you want to ask is: Which type of property is there a shortage of?

This will be directly related to the demographic profile of the area. Is there a shortage of family homes because there are more families in the area than singles? More precisely, is there a shortage of family homes near to the services families need? Are there many family homes near the local schools, shopping, parks, etc.?

It would be easier if Property Investing information was available that is neutral, informative, and comprehensive on its own. But you will more typically find huge amounts of mismatched information that needs to be sorted out and put together. If you don't take the time to do this, however, you are gambling with your hard-earned money. My award-winning (2015 Winner of the iProperty.com People's Choice Award for Best Real Estate Investment Company) Four Fundamentals Due Diligence Checklist will get you just the information you need to make the best investment decisions and minimize your risk.

With residential property, you need to discover what the relevant population in that area wants most. That's how you will make the most profit. One of the biggest growth areas of residential property over the last few years has been in student housing. This is a difficult area to classify because although it is fundamentally residential, it also a business as it specifically relies upon the schools to have a constant supply of freshman students to keep the accommodations in demand.

Personally, I prefer longer-term tenants and leverage. Student accommodation takes up too much of my capital that I can use elsewhere to buy three more properties for the same capital up front!

Business Property

When you invest in a property that has a business as a tenant you take on a whole set of new variables and, consequently, risks. If there are more things that can go wrong, you're going to have more sleepless nights.

However, if you are smart enough to hit the business property cycle right at the beginning, when new companies are moving to town and the local governments are giving grants willy-nilly, you can make a fortune. But, in terms of risk, unless you are at an expert level, I would never advise making this type of investment your first choice.

Fifty percent of new businesses in the United States fail in the first five years. I can tell you that most business landlords do not investigate their prospective business tenants anywhere near as thoroughly as they should. They don't even look at their accounts. And they suffer the consequences. If you do go this route, you'd be wise to use this checklist. (Local laws will vary regarding what information you can request, so check these first.)

Small Business Tenant Checklist
- ✓ Check audited accounts for at least three years, if possible.
- ✓ Check latest management accounts for last quarter (to see how the business is doing currently).
- ✓ Check bank account balances
- ✓ Check if the type of business they are in is growing or declining.
- ✓ Check to see if their employees are paid on time.
- ✓ Check bios of the management team.
- ✓ Check to see if they have let go of any employees lately.
- ✓ Check to see if they are involved in any kind of legal action/law suit.
- ✓ Check out who their clients are.
- ✓ Get a bank reference.
- ✓ Get a client reference.
- ✓ Insist on at least three months' rent deposit and three months' of utility bills deposit.
- ✓ Find out if the business offers attractive packages to attrack the right talent that will help the business flourish.

Finally, you want to make sure the local government is friendly to landlords and businesses (e.g., you can evict in

30 days, taxes are low both for you and business owner, etc.). You might even discover government incentives. In Cork, Ireland, a huge telemarketing/customer service industry has developed, in large part because the Irish government gave that industry a ten-year tax exemption. They did it to fight massive unemployment, and it was a win-win.

This may seem like a huge list to tackle, and most of the time you will not be able to tick everything off the list because you cannot get all the information or the business hasn't been operating long enough to have years of paperwork.

If the area is not also friendly to the type of employee that business retains, it will be harder to find a business tenant in the first place. You want to be sure the environment is one that allows businesses to flourish in your chosen town or city. If it's a business that relies on foot traffic, you want to be sure there's a market for that type of business. If it's an online or industrial business, make sure transportation and other supporting services are affordable and available.

In conclusion, this type of property is one I tread very carefully with, and again I do not recommend any of you do this until you are financially free.

A **hotel** is the one great exception in business property. In a hotel investment you can reduce your risk because you have more than one tenant—your hotel guests.

Your hotel guests give you more than one revenue stream. They can spend money in your restaurant, spa, bar, and on any other services you offer. You can create a multiple-income-stream business out of one property.

Modern-day economics prohibit most people from affording traditional hotels; however, there are now some diverse options. The "book early, stay cheaper," budget hotel model, with smaller numbers of rooms, has become a huge business. People can even buy land and rent out rooms in a mobile home on the site and call it a hotel. It does not have to involve huge capital. I have always loved the many, many ways you can enter this market.

But remember, a hotel is a business, and to make that business profitable, you have to fill the rooms and get people using and paying for your services. Therefore, you must still use the four fundamentals whenever you are thinking about this kind of property. At the end of the day, just like any other property, it has to be in demand. When you get savvier, you can buy a run-down building way below market value—as long as you have studied that development plan, looked at job growth, seen an influx of new people into that area, and other people's capital investments making it operational. Give your investors a share of it and you will then have one of the best investments you will ever own.

Land

Land has been the hallmark of property investment for thousands of years. If you own it, and you have a license to develop it into residential, commercial, or industrial enterprises, when there is a huge demand, you will make the most profit. This is simply because you are making all of the available profit on the land and the buildings on it. You are the developer; there is no third party, no chain.

Smart property developers have made fortunes from this, and they continue to do so. For the lesser mortals who are not yet developers but aspiring to be, there are great lessons to be learned.

When I was a kid the only rich person in my family was my uncle. He was the one living in the big house with the big swimming pool, driving the Rolls-Royce. In all he has owned fifteen Rolls-Royces and developed hundreds of properties under his own steam.

He is very rich and smart. He's so smart, he kept ownership of the land, which the properties were built upon, and sold the houses as leaseholds. The leasehold entitles him to charge ground rent to the homeowners in perpetuity (forever). (Leasehold is rare in the United States; the standard is freehold/fee simple.) This annual income, times hundreds of houses, gives him a huge six figure income, residual income that has enabled him to not work since he was twenty-five.

When he was twenty-five he had nothing. "How did he start?" is the burning question on your mind, isn't it? He convinced his mother to let him use her house as collateral to go a bank and borrow the money to build his first house.

He built his first house with swimming pool for £25,000. He refinanced that house a few years later for £150,000, and used the cash to buy land and develop four more houses, which he sold as leaseholds for double the profit before he even built them. He just kept doing this year after year, and was most certainly the happiest man in our small town. He will tell you himself it was not easy, because he had to spend time convincing the planning office to give him permission to develop property on the land. Many times he was refused but he kept at it and eventually got the permission he needed to make the money he wanted!

I remember him organizing rock concerts in the early 1970s, with singers such as Rod Stewart, David Bowie, Chuck Berry and many more. He got them to come to a small town called Buxton, Derbyshire, with a population of only 5,000. He sold the tickets in then Richard Branson's first Virgin Records stores all over the country and made a fortune. I was only five years old but I remember being in the back seat of his white Rolls-Royce going to a concert. Boy, that was an inspiration!

Again, I have to place a caveat on what I am writing here. I insist you must be financially free, have replaced your income with passive income, before you think about starting any kind of land venture.

Once you're in a position to take the risk and make the effort to do land deals, you have to focus on the skill of networking. You need to start meeting the people who own the land and have access to the land. Once I focused my time on finding and networking with the right people, it paid off and is still paying big dividends to me.

Finding the right land is also a skill. Land acquisition really comes down to how well you know the structure and development plan of the area: what are they going to build in the future, how are they going to improve the area, is your land likely to be included in that betterment plan?

This is why part of your networking has to be connecting with the local building authorities, the planning and zoning office, etc. All plans by developers have to be submitted and most of them are public record, which most people don't really know. What it means is you can walk into most town planning offices and ask about the future development of an area, what land is being used, and discover what land could be for sale in the area that is being developed.

Having prior knowledge of what plans are approved and what is likely to be approved is a goldmine. This information enables you to target specific areas, and even invest in existing residential property. All you have to know now is how to extract this gold.

You'll still need to start with your four fundamentals. Changing land use most definitely changes those four indicators (cycles, demographics, development plan, economic factors), sometimes hugely. That's why your basic research must always come first!

Learning and thinking about land added a golden aspect to every investment. One of my standard questions became, "What will happen to this land in the next ten years?" By asking that question I completely changed the way I invested.

In 2009, I successfully acquired five apartments in Sri Hartamas, Kuala Lumpur, Malaysia and tripled their value in four years. How?

I went to the planning office and discovered they were moving the king's palace to the area. The king of Malaysia! They had already allocated the land for it, and building would start in 2010. As soon as I had verified these facts I started buying.

A king as your neighbour creates an interesting new economy. There are palace workers and tourists, and people wanting to move into the area because the perception was that it would be safer and cleaner. And they were right! As soon as the king moved in, old roads were repaired and new and improved infrastructure was put in place.

Crowd-fund

This has become the latest hip word in investing. Crowd-funding is where you own property, a share of it, without committing all of your capital. In business, crowdfunding has helped millions of companies get off the ground and thrive. It is only good news for property investors, because it enables more people to start investing and get on the property ladder.

Crowd-funding is a strategy that helps the cycle accelerate faster as it is a low-cost investment most people can afford. Some crowdfunding opportunities start at only £1,000. I was able to complete a huge agricultural land deal in Cambodia using crowdfunding to grow different types of in-demand crops, such as cassava (tapioca), mangos, and kampot peppercorns.

A friend introduced me to the former prime minister of Cambodia (the power of your network), who owned land and had access to much more. I convinced the prime minister to put that land into a company with three other shareholders. We kept 51 percent and sold the remaining 49 percent of the company that owned the land to other investors. One share was priced at $52,000. I sold all forty-nine shares of my Cambodian company within nine hours of sending the offer to my investor circle (the power of your network).

In that offer I promised them I would give them an 85 percent profit on their investment within one year. In truth, we had already sold the first crops the land was going to produce, because we had the land researched by soil experts and we knew what we could grow and how quickly we could grow it.

I returned the 85 percent profit to my investors in nine months, three months ahead of schedule. This was a fantastic deal and, remember, I did it with no capital of my own!

When investing in any crowd-funding deal, again you must use your four fundamentals, and of course check the company out that is offering the deal. Make sure you have security when you invest, and that you can get at least 10 percent annual returns (some pay a lot more depending on how much you invest), which is ten times that of a bank savings account in most places in the world. Once you have your emergency fund in place (at least three months' salary) you have no excuse not to start investing!

10. Renovation

Here is what you must know regarding this subject. If you put money into renovating an apartment or condo, you are not going to get much return out of your dollars invested.

Why? Because you cannot increase the size of the apartment, it's already built into a building. The only thing you can do is beautify and, maybe in rare cases, knock a couple of walls through.

The best renovation profits you can make are on landed properties (houses) because you can increase the size of the house. When you have more rooms available, an office, a garage, or a swimming pool, you will by default increase the value as you have made it more than it was.

The most important rooms to invest money in are the kitchens and the bathrooms, because most people use these rooms the most and want to feel comfortable in the places they spend the most time. A sexy kitchen and bathroom can make you a lot more profit, as every buyer who is not an investor is an emotional buyer. Sometimes even one look at those rooms can sell the house at a higher price.

Beginners always complicate renovations because they think the tenant and buyer will love their taste! This is simply not true. Your best friend when doing a house up is warm white paint. Stick to neutral colors always. People can then furnish it how they like without worrying about clashing with the color of the walls.

Sometimes you don't even have to renovate. If it is well below market value, you can still make a healthy profit when you flip it. Nevertheless, you will be amazed what a good clean up and a new coat of paint can do to spruce things up, and it's very inexpensive.

11. Appraisal Confirmed and Leveraged?

A bank-approved appraisal that is well above your purchase price is critical and will help you raise more capital when you re-finance the property. You must insist on a proper appraisal; do not just take the first bank's appraisal. You will be surprised to find that appraisers will give it a different value every time.

Get the appraisal optimized to the highest possible price. This is a critical step before you put any of your own money down. If your profit margins are less than 10 percent, you are going to find it difficult. If they are at least 20 percent, you are setting yourself up very well. An optimal appraisal will enable you to leverage, borrow more, and get more cash out of the deal, which will in turn enable you to accelerate your journey to financial freedom.

I have shown you in earlier chapters how we have successfully done this with several properties in the past six months. As a reminder, here is one development we purchased in Manchester for well below the market price, and because of the appraisal we were able to go to another bank and borrow far more.

Appraisal: £1,680,000
Purchase price: £860,000
Deposit: £172,000 (raised through crowdfund deposits)
Balance: £688,000
Mortgage payment: £7,076.85 per month
Rent: £10,800 per month
<u>Refinance after six months</u>
New appraisal: £1,950,000
Refinance percentage: 70%
New mortgage amount: £1,365,000 (4.5%, 30-year term)
New mortgage payment: £6,916.25 per month
Cash out of the deal: £677,000

Is this an exceptional deal? People who are not familiar with property investing would perceive this is to be the deal of the century.

Experienced investors like me are doing deals like this every month. For us, this is normal!

And for you to enjoy the same benefits and profits as I do you just have to learn and master the *Financial Freedom Guarantee* blueprint and you will absolutely be able to do the same.

As I told you earlier, you make most of your profit when you buy a property not when you sell it. This is true because you are locking in your profits at day one, when you buy at the beginning of a cycle and at below market value.

You cannot do this at the top of a peak cycle because these deals are not available; people already purchased them long before. Now you can see how the first of the four fundamentals, the cycle, is the most important in achieving financial freedom. When you use all four fundamentals and the associated tools in unison, you will unlock all the profit you can make and more. Follow the yellow brick road—sorry, the *Financial Freedom Guarantee* blueprint—and you will absolutely succeed.

12. What is the Price range You Should Target?

This really depends on two things: a) how much deposit you can raise; and b) how much you can borrow, what mortgage you can get, from the bank. I discussed this subject at length in the previous chapter on borrowing. Refer back if you need, and remember: first things first, your credit profile.

Before you make an offer for any property, you must have all of your financing in place. Meaning, you must know what you can borrow before you buy, not after. This focuses your search laser because you will only be searching for property you know you can finance, whether it be on your own or through an investment share group. To do this, research all the banks' offers, know your net worth and then see what strategy you can use from chapter 6 to borrow even more.

When you have found something a little bit over your budget, but you know it is a fantastic deal (from all your research), you must always go to the strategies in chapter 6, and find a way to make that deal possible. It may be you have to buy with a friend to seize the opportunity and not miss out on those awesome deals.

13. What Mortgage Deal Should You Secure?

This can make or break the deal for you. Let's have a quick look at what you must optimize in the mortgage to create positive cash flow. You must have as much cash coming in as you can every month to have financial freedom.

a.   Mortgage term (length in years). The longer term the mortgage, the less the monthly payment will be and the more cash you will have every month. There are strategies to increase the length of mortgages in chapter 6.

b.   Interest rate. This must of course be as low as possible. At the beginning of cycles, interest rates are very low. As the cycle accelerates and more people buy, banks increase those rates, sometimes quite rapidly.

c.   Fixed interest term/interest only/variable interest

Most of the time, at the beginning of a cycle, interest-only mortgages are the best. That's because you're not repaying the actual capital you have borrowed, you're only paying the bank.

If you have an interest-only mortgage, please keep your eyes on the interest rate. If the interest rate increases, you will have less cash in hand at the end of the month. You must be ready to refinance when interest rates increase, and sometimes you may need to opt for a shorter-term, low fixed rate. Financial freedom is all about keeping the costs of borrowing as low as possible and receiving the highest rents you can generate.

d. Exact penalties. Also, and finally, please read the small print and know what the penalty is for refinancing before the end of the mortgage term. If you refinance too soon, you may have to pay up to a whopping 3 percent penalty of what you originally borrowed. Sometimes it may not be worth it, and you might have to delay. Just use simple calculations to compare the amount of the penalty with the amount you'll save with the better interest rate.

14. EIA and TIA.

Warning: This may look complicated! I will give a simple overview later.

These acronyms stand for Environmental Impact Assessment and Traffic Impact Assessment. Before I expand on these two reports, which are directly related to one of the four fundamentals—the development plan—I will share with you their definitions. Much more can be found online and in case studies, which are very beneficial to read.

> **EIA:** Environmental Impact Assessment is an evaluation of the likely environmental impacts of a proposed project or development, taking into account socioeconomic, cultural, and health effects.
>
> **TIA:** A Traffic Impact Assessment is a comprehensive, technical appraisal of the traffic and safety implications relating to a proposed project or development.

If you can extract these two reports on the area you are thinking of investing in you will glean information that is very powerful. It may just show you exactly why people are thinking of moving into the area or out of the area. These days, quality of life is very much dependent on where you live. If the air is polluted or the ground contaminated with toxic chemicals, it's a no-go.

The EIA studies will give you information on how the present environment is affecting the residents and, if you dig deeper, the impact of any new building projects on the horizon. If a new factory is being built in the area, for example, it could be great for jobs but really bad for residents' health.

Similarly, if the area has a great park and there are plans to build onto it, you'll need to investigate the pros and cons. The EIA can be one of the best research sub-tools you have to predict what might happen. That trip to the local planning office should be a priority.

How traffic moves in and around a town or city can be pivotal in people's decision to live there. Traffic noise is a massive deterrent. It causes stress and sleeping problems. Also in the TIA is information on how long it will take to travel to business districts by various means of transport and if there are other types of transportation available. If the commute to most jobs takes over an hour, you will have another barrier in attracting tenants or buyers.

The Financial Freedom Buyer's Guide is essential in proper pre-investment education. This is the time when you can ascertain if the money you are going to invest is going to work for you.

Now I invite you to reread chapter 3 and refresh your memory of my Four Ultimate Property Buying Fundamentals before moving on to the detailed checklist of necessary, full due diligence required for investing in your next property. Remember, every piece of relevant research you do reduces your risk of losing money.

The due diligence checklist that follows is categorized according to the four fundamentals. For each, I will give you examples of great online resources that you can start using, beginning with the house you live in right now. This will give you great practice and insight into how much information you can generate.

This checklist will be included with the Financial Freedom Buyer's Guide at: www.financialfreedomguarantee.com/buyersguide.

THE FOUR FUNDAMENTALS DUE DILIGENCE CHECKLIST

1. **Cycles.** Always invest as close to the beginning of a cycle as you can. Research:

    a. *the last transaction prices of specific units, condos, landed property and historical ten/five year past record of appreciation, depreciation:*

    UK: www.gov.uk/land-registry-transaction-data/
    www.rightmove.co.uk

    US: www.fhfa.gov/DataTools/Downloads/Pages/House-Price-Index.aspx

    Australia: stat.abs.gov.au/itt/r.jsp?databyregion

    b. bank lending rates and loan-to-value lending:

    UK: www.moneysupermarket.com/loans/

    US: www.bankrate.com/national-mortgage-rates/

    Australia: www.infochoice.com.au/home-loans.aspx

    c. price of copper: www.investing.com/commodities/copper-historical-data

    d. *first-time buyer homes, availability and affordability:*

    UK: www.gov.uk/government/policies/helping-people-to-buy-a-home/supporting-pages/help-for-first-time-buyers

    US: http://portal.hud.gov/hudportal/HUD?src=/topics/buying_a_home

    Australia: www.firsthome.gov.au

    e. stock market liquidity: www.reuters.com/finance/global-market-data

2. **Demographics/Population Growth.** Make sure there is a sustainable increase in population and understand why. Research:

    a. Area population:

    - Is it declining or increasing, at what rate, and why?

- What are the demographics, (age group, income, occupations, time poor, time rich, married, children).
- What are the psychographics? (lifestyle, CBD, beaches, student education, green, entertainment.
- Is the occupancy of building or area declining or increasing?

UK: www.ons.gov.uk/ons/guide-method/
          comendiums/compendium-of-uk-statistics/
          population-and-migration/

US: www.census.gov/popclock

Australia: www.abs.gov.au/ausstats/abs@.
          nsf/0/1647509ef7e25faaca2568a900154b63?
          opendocument

b. People's motivation for selling? Debt, divorce, or death? Face-to-face negotiation and fact finding (do not ever rely on an agent).

3. **Development Plan.** Study the construction and development plan for the area, and ensure there is massive investment in the infrastructure so your target market of renters or buyers will stay there or move there. Research:

- Local plan and city or state plan
- Developer's plan and developer's track record
- Facilities for your target market? (schools, transportation, shopping, restaurants, entertainment, parks, etc.)
- EIA and TIA (environmental impact assessment and traffic impact assessment)
- Residential zoning
- Industrial zoning
- Retail zoning
- Commercial zoning (Business)

UK: www.agma.gov.uk/cms_media/files/growth_plan_final_1_1.pdf
www.gov.uk/government/uploads/system/uploads/attachment_data/file/221014/Greater-Manchester-City-Deal-final_0.pdf

US: http://plan2020.com/plans/

Australia: www.strategy.planning.nsw.gov.au/sydney/the-plan/

- Maps.

  It is a great exercise to draw a map around your chosen property.

  The nine pieces of information on your map you need to know and should color code:

  1. Residential areas.
  2. Commercial business areas. (Special allocation for new business, training centers, etc.)
  3. Industrial/factory areas.
  4. Environmental areas (parks and greenery).
  5. Shopping and retail areas.
  6. Infrastructure for education (areas of schools and colleges, etc.).
  7. Infrastructure for transportation (road, rail, airport, bus networks).
  8. Infrastructure for utilities and services (government services, welfare, water, electric, community centers, etc.
  9. Infrastructure for cultural pursuits (places of worship, museums, theaters, special allocation, etc.).

     https://earth.google.com/
     https://maps.google.com/
     www.walkscore.com

4. **Economic Factors (Job Growth).** Make sure employment opportunities in the area are abundant and likely to be abundant for a long time to come. Make sure it's easy for companies and entrepreneurs to do business there and that you have a friendly local government. Research:

   a. business growth in the area

   - Which business segment is growing?
   - Is there enough business talent to fill jobs?
   - Business grants
   - Government investment into new and existing businesses
   - Entrepreneurial investment
   - Business costs (office space rents, etc.)
   - College or university presence in job growth
   - Foreign investment

   UK: www.businessgrowthhub.com

   US: www.indychamber.com/economic-development/why-indianapolis

   c. friendly government (property tax and other tax) and fiscally sound government?

   UK: www.globalpropertyguide.com/Europe/United-Kingdom/Taxes-and-Costs

   US: www.globalpropertyguide.com/North-America/United-States/Taxes-and-Costs

   Australia: www.globalpropertyguide.com/Pacific/Australia/Taxes-and-Costs

That is pretty much it in terms of research. It will never be perfect, so don't stress if you simply cannot find certain information. It is in the gathering and understanding that information that you'll find the critical success factor in your purchase.

And now, in the next chapter, it's time to crunch some numbers that will get you ever closer to your goal of financial freedom.

CHAPTER 8
DO THE NUMBERS

hen you are ready to acquire great returning assets, and you know how to spot them, thanks to the award-winning research strategies you have mastered, it's time to crunch the numbers. There are only five numbers you need to know to ensure you are investing in the right property.

Many people at this stage fall in love with a property, and they fail to complete this part of the investment process. Such behavior will keep you poor and working forever. Should you lose your job, which could happen at any time, and be unable to pay your mortgage, you will be financially incarcerated with no place to hide except six years of bad credit. So please read this section very carefully and get it right. Each property you buy from now on will set you free from the rat race!

The first thing I am going to do here is to show you a case study. Do not worry if it is not in your currency or price range, it's just to help you calculate.

<u>Property Purchase Example</u>
Purchase price: $500,000
Monthly rent: $3,000
Annual rent: $36,000
Appraisal: $600,000
Deposit: $50,000
Mortgage (90%): $450,000
Mortgage term: 25 years
Monthly mortgage payment: $2,500
Annual mortgage payments: $30,000
Renovation cost: $25,000
Annual capital appreciation (estimated, for 5 years): 15%

To calculate simple yield, or the gross percentage you will make, before costs are deducted, use this formula:

Annual rent ÷ Purchase price x 100 = % yield
So, using our example purchase:
$36,000 ÷ $500,000 x 100 = 7.2

This first calculation tells you immediately how much cash you can generate every month from the property you are investing in. Less important is how much the property will gain in value. Whatever gain there is won't be cash until you liquidate it. This means you cannot spend that cash yet, and if you cannot spend it, you can't use it to replace your salary.

The cash this property generates every month is $3,000 a month, giving you a 7.2 percent return on your money. This, remember, is the gross amount.

What we really need to know is how much money is going into your pocket at the end of the month, your net cash flow. So the next calculation is the most important one.

To calculate net cash flow yield, or the percentage that will go in your pocket), use this formula:

Annual rent – Annual mortgage payments x 100 = % Net cash flow
So, using our example purchase:
$36,000 - $30,000 ÷ $500,000 x 100 = 1.2

A 1.2 percent return on your investment would give you, after paying the mortgage, $6,000 a year or $500 per month. A net yield of 1.2 percent is the bare minimum I would work with. Anything below that is just a waste of time and your precious cash resources. If your salary is $3,000 a month, you would need to buy six of these houses to fire your boss and replace your salary. That is more difficult than buying three or four, so always look to get the most cash out of the deal per month as you can.

There are two ways you can do this: either extend the length of the mortgage so the monthly payment is lower, as discussed in earlier chapters; or look for better BMV (below market value), lower-cost properties at the beginning of cycles with great fundamentals like those I have shared earlier in this book. Or you could do both. You can see once you do the first round of number crunching, you can look at getting a better mortgage with the bank and negotiate a lower price with the seller.

If you have read my book carefully, you are already pre-approved by the banks to buy this house, as you have all your paperwork in place. In my case I can raise a bridge loan in twenty-four hours to capture a property, so I can always say to the seller, "I have the cash waiting, I am a cash buyer," and you can show them the proof.

When sellers see you are that serious and they don't have to wait months to get their money, they become highly motivated to sell even if they are getting less money. It is better to get 90 percent of what they want now than 100 percent of what they want in two years or never. Available money in days is a massive motivator!

Now let's look at gross yield or value from the deal. Use this formula:

Initial appraisal + Annual rent – Purchase price ÷ Purchase price x 100 = % Gross yield

So:

$600,000 + $36,000 - $500,000 ÷ $500,000 x 100 = 27.2

This, of course is a great number, and it shows you the actual return of the property in its first year. It means you have locked in a 27.2 percent gross profit already.

This is because you purchased the property nearly 20 percent below the market value. Remember as I told you earlier, you make all of your money on property when you buy it, not when you sell it. So you must focus on capturing as much profit as you can on day one. Let's look at this gross profit again in the years ahead.

We made an assumption that the property value would increase by 15 percent per year over the next five years due to the diligent research we did using our four fundamentals and the Due Diligence Checklist. Using the new value after one year, the formula is:

New value + Annual rent – Purchase price ÷ Purchase price (or loan balance) x 100 = New % gross yield

So:

$690,000 + $36,000 - $500,000 ÷ $500,000 x 100 = 45.2

Does this happen in real life? You betcha! And, sometimes it goes way beyond the figures I have shown here.

By the second year, the property value has risen 15 percent to $690,000, because all your fundamentals are firing. Now you can do a new gross yield calculation to see how much "in the money" you are a year later!

The only number that has changed is the value. When your rent starts to increase and your loan from the bank decreases, you are even more in the money. I do however, have to state, you are only truly in the money when you can use the money. This is the difference between people who are financially free, and people who keep holding on because of greed, and end up losing money in the correction cycle.

From the second year onwards you can easily refinance your property and get quite a lot of capital out of it. In this case you can likely refinance up to 90 percent of the value: $690,000 x 90% = $621,000.

You will now have another $121,000 of extra capital ($621,000 - $500,000 = $121,000).

When you get your research right and your financing right, in one exercise you can buy two more properties and create enough passive income to replace your salary and fire your boss! This is how it's done, ladies and gentlemen! This is how you break free from the shackles of people telling what you to do, banks controlling you, and governments failing you.

Permission is now granted to live your life!

This next calculation starts to show you how very sexy property investing really is. This shows you, like a smack in the face, what you get back for your deposit money, a.k.a., your gross deposit yield.

Annual rent ÷ Deposit paid x 100 = Gross deposit % yield
So:
$36,000 ÷ $50,000 x 100 = 72

In this case after one year, your $50,000 has generated $36,000 in cash flow! Yes, it's amazing, where else you can get that return in such a short time?

In 2014 the Dow Jones only managed 7.5 percent! That is almost ten times what the Dow Jones did, and I have not even included the capital gain, only the rental yield. This, of course is the gross amount. But even when we take the costs out and get to the next calculation, the net cash flow return, or net deposit yield, is still very impressive.

Annual rent − Annual mortgage payments ÷ Deposit x 100 = Net deposit % yield

So:

$36,000 - $30,000 ÷ $50,000 x 100 = 12

You are getting 12 percent cash on cash! With money in the bank, you would be getting between 0.5 percent and 3 percent (if you're really lucky) but you wouldn't own a property and you certainly wouldn't be enjoying any capital gain from your money. As you can see, keeping it in the bank is the worst thing you can do.

Next, let's look at what happens if you decide to sell this property at the end of the second year. It is always important to do net yields and returns because this shows you realistically what cash you can earn and get back from the property. If you have your four fundamentals criteria all kicking ass, you really do not want to sell any earlier, because you will miss out on so many profits. By merely waiting a few years, all your money worries are over!

Annual rent (2 years) − Annual mortgage payments (2 years) + Capital appreciation (2 years) ÷ Purchase price x 100 = Net % yield of sale

So:

($72,000 - $60,000) + $190,000 ÷ $500,000 x 100 = 40.4

In this case, at an appreciation rate of 15 percent per year, you are going to make $196,000 over a twenty-four-month period. The reasons you are making this: 1) You purchased the property below market value, for only $500,000, and now it is worth $690,000; 2) you have collected two years of rent, or $12,000 after mortgage payments.

You have a clear cash profit of $202,000 should you decide to sell at year two. That's over 40 percent returns!

And finally, we can do a renovation calculation. Renovation can be a clever strategy; however, like any other strategy you have to know when to use it and what to do. And if you have noticed, I have not included renovation in my award-winning Due Diligence Checklist, simply because it does not perform as well as other things.

Also, as I mentioned before, if you do renovation on an apartment or condominium you are not going to get much return back. Why? Because you cannot increase the size of that property, so you cannot generate a higher appraisal. Higher appraisals come when you can increase the size of houses and make use of the land it has available.

With that in mind, if you can get hold of a rundown property with all the four fundamentals spot on (cycle; development plan; population; economic factors), you can make a fortune when you renovate.

And any renovation you do on a big scale needs a really good architect. These are the necessary people when the building is substantial and you are making significant structural improvements. Here's a formula for renovation yield, still using the same property example. Assume we spent $25,000 on the renovation and had it appraised immediately afterward for an increase in value of $90,000:

Difference in appraisals – Renovation costs ÷ Purchase price x 100 = Renovation yield (%)

So:

$90,000 - $25,000 ÷ $500,000 x 100 = 13

It is important to have it re-appraised immediately after; do not wait long. By doing this you can borrow more, and accelerate your journey to financial freedom.

Before you do any renovation, a good exercise is to compare selling prices of renovated properties in the area with the un-renovated ones. This will help you see what's best to do, in terms of remodeling. But stick to my guide of neutral colors and great kitchens and bathrooms (where people spend most of their time).

I have seen many renovation projects, done at the right time (cycle), double and triple the price of the property. I have seen more renovations done at the wrong time lead to people losing more than half their money.

This is why you must follow the blueprint step-by-step and never assume you have found the holy grail of property projects. Research, research, research!

One last thing I will mention in this chapter is associated legal and closing costs. You must analyze these carefully in order to ensure you can finance the whole project. Generally these costs run between 2 percent and 4 percent of the property price. This is why it is essential you have a great lawyer on board to ensure the property is clear of any encumbrance (liens, etc.) on the property and the land is free and clear.

CHAPTER 9
MANAGE YOUR INVESTMENTS WISELY

P eople ask me constantly, "What if I acquire an asset that is not in my country, and a pipe bursts and I have to go and fix it?" You would think this is a major issue, and it can be if you do not know how to get your properties managed properly. Investment management can be the difference between a nightmare and a dream. You'll discover here how my properties never give me any problems, and I haven't even seen many of them.

First, of course, you have to have a damn good management company with a great track record of managing other properties in the region in which you are buying. Equally important and less obvious is that you must have a tenant in that property, even if you have not purchased or completed the purchase yet.

You must also ensure that it is very easy to find another tenant, so that if one leaves, others are literally queuing up to move in. And not just any old tenant: a tenant that is prequalified, can afford the rent and can afford to keep paying it.

I know this may sound disconnected, but the major reason I am able to get quality tenants is because I buy quality property using my award-winning four fundamentals (cycle, development plan, population, economic factors). They are the foundation to the ten-step blueprint for financial freedom: You must follow my ten steps precisely!

Once you have identified the property using the four fundamentals, get the tenant. If it is the right property, a tenant should already be in there; however, you have to make sure that the tenant is a good one. Ask the buyer to provide proof the tenant is paying on time and what amount. And if they are good tenant, why change them?

If the property comes with a good tenant, they will still have to sign a new agreement with you when you become the new, legal owner. When you have taken ownership insist on a meeting with the tenant to get to know them and, more importantly, find out how long they intend to stay. If they are planning to leave within a year, you need to find a new tenant immediately, to discover if your property is easy to rent and also to minimize your risk of gaps in tenancy. You don't want that, as that will adversely affect your cash flow.

MEET THE PROPERTY MANAGERS IN YOUR TARGETED AREA.

I would insist you contact every property manager in your area, before you commit any funds to the property.

Every action you take before you buy is to minimize your risk. Please do not forget how long it took you to save up for your deposit, and how easily you could lose it if you buy the wrong property. Most people are only able to buy one property in a lifetime, maybe two if they are very fortunate. But if you make mistakes now, you could lose everything you have worked for.

If you cannot meet the property managers face to face, a phone call is the next best option. And follow up with e-mails; ask them how many properties they have rented successfully, and how many they are managing currently.

As an extra precaution, it is prudent and really a must to go online and check their reputation (see checklist that follows). As I said before, especially if you live far away, beware managers charging you crazy amounts for: new refrigerators or other appliances, unnecessary maintenance, and false break-ins. The farther away you live, the more confidence they will have in ripping you off.

I cannot emphasize enough how important a good management company is. You must guarantee the money reaches you and is not sabotaged along the way! Heed these tips.

MANAGEMENT COMPANY CHECKLIST

1. Ensure that the company is properly licensed and registered with the local governing authority.

In developed countries this has been happening for a while, and it is generally well monitored; however, it does not mean it's perfect by any means at all. You still have to check that licenses are current and make sure they haven't had any complaints against them.

In places like Malaysia, they have only started licensing real estate agents and management companies this past year. In those situations, you have to be extra careful.

2. Check out their track record with other properties in the same area.

Visit or contact the company in question and get a listing of what properties they manage and how long they have managed them. Ask the agency if you can speak to five owners, at least, who have their properties with them. They might hesitate because of privacy issues, but this can be worked out. It's called getting references.

3. Check their online reputation.

Do a thorough search of the manager's name and the company name. Look for complaints and landlord feedback. You will be surprised what you can find.

If you find some really juicy information, try and call the complainant. Please also bear in mind, online is not the most accurate source for good information, as business competitors pretend and make fake complaints. This does happen a lot, and you will know if it is fake, because when you speak to the complainant they will not give you their contact details and not be able to give you the address of the property they supposedly own.

4. Test them! Get them to find you a tenant even though you have not purchased the property yet.

This is probably the best way you can get the truth. If none of the companies have found you a tenant within a month, the property you are thinking of buying has serious holes in it.

5. Put an advert in the local paper and find yourself a tenant!

This costs very little, and really is your final check. Because you cannot trust anybody to tell you they have tried.

If nobody is answering your ad after four low-cost insertions, one of two things are happening; either the rent is too high or there is something wrong with your property and you have not done your research properly!

6. Ensure you understand their eviction procedures.

Every property management company will disclose their eviction procedures, which should follow the law to the letter. In some parts of the world, it will cost a fortune to evict a non-paying tenant and it could take years. In the US city of Indianapolis, Indiana, as I mentioned I can remove a tenant thirty days after non-payment of rent. The local sheriff will visit the property and remove them.

But most of it comes down to how the tenancy agreement is structured, which I have explained in earlier chapters.

7. Be diligent, find a good management company.

It may be tempting to avoid the fees of property management and do it yourself. But one of the true secrets to financial freedom is to never manage your own properties. If you do, eventually it becomes a full-time job. Financial freedom is about having the time to do the things you really love, not responding to a tenant's phone call that the pipe burst. Outsource it. I do not manage any of my properties personally.

You are welcome to ask my help desk for advice, as long as you're a subscriber of course. My members come first, and I look after them. That is why I was winner of the iProperty.com People's Choice Awards in the category of Best Real Estate Investment Company, 2014–2015. People love how we look after them and get them the returns they need to create financial freedom. To be an official subscriber please go this link and sign up for free: www.financialfreedomguarantee.com. Also make sure you follow me on Facebook for daily inspiration, follow me on youtube for educational free videos and follow me on Instagram to see how a financial freedom lifestyle really looks. You can also follow my blog at: www.datoserimarcorobinson.me Put it this way, I wish I had had me (with all I know now) when I was starting out. It would have made my journey to achieve my financial goals much faster!

A NOTE ON INSURANCE

As a landlord you must have it. I insist. Anything can happen and you must be covered for the damage. Some people regard this as just an unnecessary extra cost. Well, I have seen enough to never be without it.

One of my students once cancelled the insurance on a house he owned (without consulting me) and a week later a big tree fell on his roof. It caused $20,000 worth of damage, which the insurance would have covered. He has never made the same mistake again. Make sure you have excellent homeowner's insurance on any property you own, and never let it lapse.

MANAGING THE RENTAL INCOME

When you are investing in other countries, it is a good idea to have bank accounts in those countries. The rent can then be then deposited, in that country's currency, into your account directly and you can access the funds online.

But do not just transfer the money to your home account at the end of each month. Wait until the exchange rate is at its most favorable. This way, you can make money off of the funds transfer between countries as well!

The only question you should be asking now is for your accountant: how can you best minimize your tax exposure? This is a question you need an answer for when you reach a threshold of three properties or more.

I made over $10 million in profits last year and only paid $35,000 in taxes. And I did it legally!

Don't be afraid of paying taxes, you have to do it. But because I own companies in different countries, I can write off many of my expenses legitimately. My advice is to consult with an expert on international tax on how to structure your business and assets.

Also I offer free videos and workshops on this subject for subscribers, just in case you wanted to hear from someone who is already financially free (which means, remember, that I am qualified to advise you!).

In summary, you must manage your investments and manage your money. I can't put it any better than the following quote I keep sharing with you: Poor people spend their money first and save what they have left. Rich people invest their money first and spend what they have left. And for your information, whenever I receive money, my default thinking is, "What can I invest this money in now?" It's not "What can I spend this money on?" Investment gives me the returns to spend on my lifestyle, but I still own the investment and it keeps paying me.

Which way would you rather be?

CHAPTER 10

CALCULATE AND MINIMIZE YOUR RISK

There is no reward without taking some risk. You just have to calculate that risk. In capturing massive wealth you must protect your gains and minimize your risk level at all times. So you must know what risk really is.

The law of financial freedom states that you must borrow money and you must leverage. However, you must only do this under a certain set of conditions, which are set in stone.

Let me remind you what this book really is: It's a ten-step blueprint that tells you how to replace your salary (living costs) with passive income (having assets that pay you an income whether you are working or not), through intelligent investment so that you can fire your boss and live life on your terms.

In this book I have explained in detail nine of those ten steps, steps you must follow exactly—no shortcuts. You must take that journey toward eventually mastery. The short-term pain of some hard-ass work in learning pays off with long-term happiness and freedom forever.

I think that's a very small price to pay, and I have said many times in this book that if you do the work in these ten steps, even with no present assets or money in the bank, you can achieve financial freedom within two years. I am prepared to underwrite that statement by guaranteeing it. How?

If you are not financially free after two years of constantly studying this book and consistently executing the steps in this book, I will give you the cost of this book back *plus* any interest you would have made in my award-winning, fully regulated property crowdfund program. In fact, I will give you my highest return of 24 percent annually on the cost of this book, so if it cost you $30, I will give you a total of $58. 80.

What you have to do is prove to me you followed all the ten steps in this book closely. Because if you want a refund after two years because you think this book did not work for you, I will give you an exam on what you learned in this book. In order to pass, you must get 50 percent correct. Why such a low pass rate? Because even if you followed half of what's in this book, you would be halfway to financial freedom by then!

I stand by my guarantee, and I disclaim anything you did in those two years that was not from the ten steps of my blueprint in this book. Because I am telling you now, it won't work—unless you win the lottery, as I said, and even then 70 percent of lottery winners end up broke within seven years.

STEP 1: DO NOT LISTEN TO UNQUALIFIED FINANCIAL ADVICE.

If you listen to government advice and listen to people who are not financially free your risk of not being financially free is calculated at 100 percent. To minimize your risk, follow step one at all times, even with family and close friends, because if they are not financially free you are not going to be either!

STEP 2: REPROGRAM YOUR DEFAULT OPERATING SYSTEM

If you do not upgrade your mindset and start programing in new financial freedom habits, you will go back to your old lack-of-money habits at light speed. And your risk of not being financially free is again very easy to calculate—it will be 100 percent! To minimize your risk, only learn new money habits from people that are already financially free.

STEP 3: GET THIS REVOLUTIONARY, EFFECTIVE FINANCIAL EDUCATION.

If you do not educate yourself on a constant basis, and I mean on a daily basis, about the mindset and mechanics (strategies) of financially free people, forget wealth, and be poor, it's a certainty. Risk Level: 100 percent.

To minimize your risk, learn to decode relevant financial information that has the certainty to set you financially free. Then, understand it, experience it by executing your strategies preferably with a qualified mentor for feedback along the way. A mentor will reduce your risk immensely and they are not expensive, but please make sure they're qualified (ask me, I know them all).

STEP 4: HAVE COMPELLING LIFE GOALS.

If you do not know what to do with your time when you are not working, you will go straight back to work and sabotage any further opportunity to be rich. Risk level, again: 100 percent.

To minimize your risk, spend time in a quiet space with absolutely no distractions (no phone, no laptop, no family, no pets, no children, no social media, nobody knocking at the door). Think clearly what you want and what you would really love to do if you had the time. To achieve this you must ask great questions to yourself in your quiet space, such as: "What do I really love to do" and "If I got paid not to go to work, what would I most love to do every day?" and "What can I do in my free time that will serve me and others best?"

Powerful questions always receive powerful answers. But only ask them in silence.

STEP 5: MASTER PRECISE MONEY ALLOCATION (PMA).

If you do not invest your money the right properties in the right places, you will lose in a big way. Follow my award-winning research plan and allocate your money in the precise spots where your money will perform. Risk level of not putting your money in the right places: 100 percent-plus! (Because you will lose more than you put in.)

To minimize your risk, analyze world markets, explore where the cycles are beginning, use your research tools. Identify targets and research without leaving any stone unturned.

STEP 6: BORROW.

To be financially free you have to borrow. If you don't borrow, once you have identified your investment targets, you will be limited in what you can buy and will never be financially free. You simply will not create enough positive cash flow. Risk Level: 100 percent.

To minimize the risk of investing learn my nine strategies of how to borrow successfully and always work on improving your credit score. Learn the bank's process of lending and how they want to reduce their risk of lending to you. Then through your research, set up bank accounts and companies in other countries in beginning cycles and create a good credit profile in those places, so you can borrow internationally. The more you can borrow, the more you will be able to do what you love to do. Because you will have more cash flow.

STEP 7: MASTER PRECISE RESEARCH ANALYSIS (PRA).

If you do not use my award-winning research tools to pinpoint the best opportunities and get the best performing properties, you are taking the biggest risk of all. Risk level: 100 percent-plus-plus. (You could lose everything and end up bankrupt from the debt of buying the wrong properties with no tenants.)

To minimize your risk significantly, discover where the beginning cycles are in different countries. Learn where populations are growing and the reasons behind it, study the structure and development plans to see what's being built and if they're investing in the area to make it better. Find out if jobs are being created and where, what kind of pay they offer, and if the businesses are sustainable.

STEP 8: DO THE NUMBERS.

If you don't know how much cash the property is giving you every month and what it is potentially going to give you in the future, including capital gain, you are blind. So many people make huge mistakes here and buy properties they love rather than properties that return great cash flow. Risk level: 100 percent-plus (as you could make the mistake of buying a negatively geared property, where the mortgage cost is higher than the rental's return).

To minimize your risk substantially here, use the many example calculations in this book. Know your numbers precisely before going in to negotiate your property purchase. Remember, to be financially free, you have to positive cash flow. I don't mean $100 per month. Using my ten steps, you should be able to buy three or four properties and retire financially free from the passive income they provide you. Look for properties that give a minimum 1.2 percent net cash flow return!

STEP 9: MANAGE YOUR INVESTMENTS WISELY.

Make your investments "hands free" and truly experience financial freedom! If you have to repair your own houses, if you are not insured, if you have chosen the wrong management company and they've put bad tenants in your property, your life will be a living hell. You will have a new full-time job being a slave to your properties! Emotional risk level: off the charts! Financial risk level: horrible!

To minimize your risk, both emotionally and financially, follow my guide on sourcing the top management companies and real estate agencies; it will truly save your life. The only job you'll have is checking your online bank accounts for the rental deposits. And when you see them, I am telling you, you'll have reached nirvana!

STEP 10: CALCULATE AND MINIMIZE YOUR RISK.

Enough said! Follow my ten steps and repeat—to be guaranteed the life you deserve, the life you always wanted, the life that's waiting for you. Then and only then will you experience the thrill, like I do, of being able to help others achieve the same financial freedom as you. And that, my friends, is when your life begins!

For more information, please visit:
www.financialfreedomguarantee.com
To see more about Marco Robinson, please visit:
www.marcorobinson.com

ABOUT THE AUTHOR

Marco is a #1 bestselling author of two books, an *Award Winning Entrepreneur & Winner of the People's Choice Best Real Estate Investment Company 2015*, a *Disruptive Philanthropist* and recently as a Restaurateur Winner of the Tatler's Best Restaurants 2015 for his NAKED restaurant concept.

He has made countless national radio and TV appearances and has spoken at the prestigious Napoleon Hill International Conference, the Ogilvy DO Debates, Bloomberg, and Forbes. He is in high demand on the speaking circuit and is invited to talk on various platforms around the globe with appearances in print newspapers including the *Telegraph*, *The Independent* and *The Daily Mail*, High Flying magazine publications including FLYBE, City Airport Magazines, TV talk shows and Prime Time TV slots.

He is the FIRST Entrepreneur to give away one of his properties FOR FREE with no mortgage in a free entry competition! This has gone viral, worldwide.

He is also the founder of the NAKED Group of Companies including the Award Winning Naked Restaurant & Bar (WINNING

TATLER'S BEST RESTAURANTS 2015) recently opened in Kuala Lumpur, Malaysia (see www.nakedrestaurantkl.com, which has already spawned three new Franchise Companies, NAKED COFFEE; NAKED PIZZA, NAKED Beauty Bars, specializing in Revolutionary one of a kind Eyelash, Nail & Spray Tan Treatments, now OPENED in the UK.

He launched another disruptive business...NKDb by 4th Base Cosmetics, a brand new cosmetics company taking the market by storm with truly not tested on animal products, no parabens and non-comedogenic, especially founded to help young women entrepreneurs. See www.4thbasecosmetics.com

And yet another new venture, a travel disruptor company, NAKED TRAVEL a fully licensed ABTA and ATOL bonded travel agency where travelers can buy their holidays in advance and save thousands of pounds. See www.naked.travel

He has built several multi-million dollar companies from scratch such as the Wealth Revolution Group, Create Demand Incentive Programs, The New Rich List, Naked restaurants, as well as raising over $30 million through a brand new award winning property Crowdfund. He develops and invests in below market value properties and shares the profits with his investors.

He personally owns over 200 properties and is now a property developer in his own right making him a self-made millionaire many times over.

He is a world authority speaker on investing, entrepreneurship and financial freedom, and he has his own FOUNDATION serving underprivileged children and female single parents, his one dream to give back after his own difficult childhood. He speaks worldwide to hundreds and thousands of people...

HOW HIS INSPIRATIONAL STORY ALL STARTED...

Marco's childhood was traumatic, at 2 years old his mum left his Dad, due to his addiction to gambling. Every week his mum would have to work four jobs just to pay the housekeeping bills and put food on the table while his Dad blew his whole salary on the horses.

Marco and his Mum would regularly move from town to town, school to school and not really make any friends, sometimes they had to sleep in the park quite often to survive... Then his Mum unfortunately entered (unbeknown to her at the time) an abusive relationship in the hope at first there would be stability.

However it regularly turned violent and they were on the road again. Marco didn't really have any schooling and left his last school at 16 without any academic qualifications, getting a cleaning job and sharing a friend's house to survive.

His Mum found the right guy eventually, but through all his challenges as a kid, he knew he was the only person who could take responsibility for his own life...he moved from job to job, to eventually settle in direct sales, the last place he imagined.

He was the worst salesperson, as he simply had no confidence at all, until one day he met the top salesman, and the top salesman said to him... "You have something inside of you, some fire, you have real talent, you can't see it, I do, I want you to read this book I read that helped me overcome my fears, but tell no-one, just read it and read it again until you get the message".

Marco read the book 8 times and became the TOP Salesperson, he had so much confidence, he told his first clients he was going to sell them timeshare today, they told him no, four hours later, they bought and handed over £10,000. Marco was so shocked at his first success EVER he was compelled to ask his buyers why they bought from him... they told him, because we saw that you believed it, so we wanted it.

He never forgot that moment…and went on to succeed, way beyond his own expectations and not without tremendous struggle, but he was familiar with struggle and discovered that it was his greatest strength…

Although he reached the top of the corporate world, he lost his job, and struggled to become an entrepreneur with no salary, and no savings as he blew his savings on the stock market. He tried and tried to succeed in business in his own, and managed to win some small contracts that kept him going…

However, after trying many times to save his marriage, it collapsed in 2008, and he was on his own, all he had was a 20 year old Volvo and an old laptop…

Then he decided it was about time, he wrote the book he always dreamed about writing. He wrote a book about his life that became a number one bestseller, *Close the Deal & Suddenly Grow Rich.*

When it became number one, he was again shocked to the core, he wrote it based on his past success as a salesperson and selling a billion dollars worth of products in ten years, but the book royalties were not enough to even survive on his own…then one day he asked a simple question "How can I become a millionaire in my own right?"…

He kept asking that same question again and again and again and one day completely out of the blue…he thought of a revolutionary idea that made him a personal fortune of $12 million in 2009.

Ever since then, because of his previous terrible record with money, he focused on how he could get money to work for him, instead of having to work for money, he hired millionaire successful financial mentors, he threw himself into the subject of money, determined to find the best way he could increase his wealth so he never had to worry about money again…

He succeeded again…this time in real estate and especially investment property. He discovered that property had a distinctive cycle, he discovered that property could create positive cash-flow, and it could easily and safely replace anyone's salary, it could, as a light bulb went off in his head, allow anybody to do what they LOVE to do, instead of working 70 hours a week and never seeing their family, and do what they had to do to pay the bills…

He got so good at property investment, friends asked him to share his success publicly and he started conducting free workshops on how to create a new income that could mean you didn't have to work again…At his first seminar, people queued right outside his office, so many people, he could not start his seminar for another hour…

Overwhelmed by the response, not just by the attendance of hundreds of people, but the standing ovation he received after he shared his life story and success, he knew this was what he really was here to do, he had found his purpose, his calling, and still today, that passion and love wows his audience and inspires them to create new income streams and fire their boss…

But it wasn't just the speaking and sharing that propelled him. He got really passionate about what makes money work harder and through his focus and study started predicting years ahead what would happen to property markets all over the world…

He got so good he had FRONT PAGE space and feature stories in International Newspapers about his success at predicting global property trends and developed four Award Winning Research Tools to help other people do the same…

He calls it, the NEW Retirement Plan, and his latest book, *The Financial Freedom Guarantee*, is the result of that work that WON him the very prestigious Accolade of People's Choice Best Real Estate Investment Company 2014/15.

But his favorite work has always been helping the underprivileged, especially in making a HUGE DIFFERENCE to people's lives, that's why he set up his own foundation, one of the best things he did was help get guide dogs into Malaysia for the blind, where they were never allowed before. He did this by helping produce and finance a movie called "Are You Blind?" which can be seen on Youtube. It went viral and that movie caused a huge movement of people to outcry the mistreatment of blind people…that eventually enabled the approval of Guide Dogs in Public Places in Malaysian History…More on his Foundation work can be found here…

https://marcorobinson.com/https://marcorobinson.com/

https://marcorobinson.com/

https://marcorobinson.com/

At the same time he was knighted for his work and his contribution to Humanity, Awarded with the honor and title of Dato' Seri Marco Robinson S.T.M.P.

To learn more about his life, seminars, courses and opportunities to work with him go to www.marcorobinson.comhttp://www.marcorobinson.com/

http://www.marcorobinson.com/

HOW TO MAKE BIG MONEY IN PROPERTY: THE JOINT VENTURE

The picture below shows the fourth property I purchased in 2015, a fifty-one-unit apartment block in Manchester, before it was fully developed. This is popularly known as "off-plan." It is now finished and fully furnished, but we sold this property before it was completed—therefore raising the money necessary from the buyers of the fifty-one individual units. However, we still own the freehold, which means we can collect ground rent from our buyers every year and still collect a healthy yield.

Before I could of even dream of doing this kind of deal, I had to buy three other apartment blocks, get financing for them in bridge loans and eventually re-mortgage them using a traditional bank with a commercial mortgage. For your information, obtaining a commercial mortgage through a company is very tax beneficial as the cost of managing and maintaining the property can be deducted from your tax bill.

Also in the United States, you can apply a 1031 tax exchange law to defer the tax of any asset you sell, and reinvest the profits into another asset within six months of the sale. This is one of the many strategies Warren Buffet has used to pay minimal tax over his many years as an investor; indeed, the tax laws are very favorable to investors, so much more so than employees, as we have already discussed in this book.

Because we had demonstrated we had successfully purchased three other apartment blocks in the United Kingdom, the developer was willing and actually excited to embark on a joint venture deal with us, where they undertook all the construction of the property while we marketed and sold it. The time period of this process? Sold out within ninety days!

Why did we sell out in ninety days? Did the investor get a great deal? Well, here's the deal guys: a truly great deal is when everybody wins and where the value proposition to each party is compelling enough to go through and close the deal.

The individual buyers were able to secure a property in the most happening property market in the world with the best fundamentals—literally all four of my award winning research tools on fire, beginning cycle, huge population increases, unprecedented infrastructure, billions of dollars of investment and sustainable, brilliant Job growth in trending industries—literally a "no-brainer" of a deal to all concerned. And because this was an off-plan deal, it was a 25 percent below-market property price to the investor, as when a property is finished and released into the market, the price increases to reflect the market demand and the newness of the build in an area where there are not many new builds at all. Our profit as joint venture partners? $2.5 million in ninety days! That, my friends, is big money…

Now I don't have to tell you all this. I could keep it secret, I could say well, you know what, you don't need to know that, that is my business. However, that's not my way of doing business at all.

I believe in collaborating and joining forces at every opportunity, because this really is the same concept as one of my buying strategies— "sharing" a purchase, where it is better to have a percentage of something than a percentage of nothing.

This concept is probably the most powerful strategy in my arsenal simply because I can accelerate the expansion of my empire and, most importantly, income, without committing all of my financial resources. I can use partners to leverage my purchases! I am very happy to say I now offer this opportunity to my students, and quite a few of them have already successfully entered into multi-property investment deals with me and made more money than they would have dreamed. I opened the door, people flooded in; I found the properties, people profited, and so did I!

To end this chapter, I must tell you about two very important resources you absolutely must have to succeed as a property investor and be financially free:

1. **A brilliant legal team**
2. **A brilliant accounting and auditing team**

Why the legal team? To execute any property transaction you must have a super lawyer that knows property law so well the strategies in this book are second nature. If you have to explain a deal twice to a lawyer, walk out of that office and never return.

Great lawyers can help you negotiate deferred exchange and completion contracts, which is essential to cash flow. Yes, they also complete their due diligence to ensure your property title is free and clear of encumbered loans by previous owners and many other important details. But when you start hitting big deals, the contracts that stipulate you can stagger the deposit payments until the property is sold to other parties are the most important for you to be living the life of your dreams. Don't even think about entering a purchase until you have the right lawyer to do the job. I would be happy to recommend one at no cost when you subscribe at www.financialfreedomguarantee.com by sending in your book purchase receipt.

Next, why the accounting team? One of the questions I get asked probably more than any question is, "What about taxes?" I even get asked this question when people are buying their first-ever property! Where taxes are either nonexistent or negligible.

People who say accountants are expensive are clearly not making very much money at all. I pay my accountants thousands, yet they have saved me millions! I really don't have to tell you, get one, it will be one of the best decisions you will ever make if you want to follow my blueprint and get into multiple property investments. When you start buying more, you make more profit, but pay relatively less tax! Interesting isn't it?

That's why again I will tell you, the rich own companies and the poor work for companies.

Not bad for one year is it? And in only the first year in operation!

I have companies all over the world, and I am able to legally save tax by owning properties in different countries using these companies as vehicles.

Remember I used to sleep on a park bench with my mum, so don't you ever think I don't care about the underprivileged! I work my heart out for them because I was there. So get off your ass and start moving and shaking, and now and again do the twist. (For the people reading this who have no idea what the twist is, go to a techno concert or edm and get in the mood; you might see me DJ-ing there.)

My final word—I quote someone from times gone by:

"If everyone did what they were capable of doing they would astound themselves."

—**Thomas Edison**

And I have the life where I astound myself every single day.

DO IT!

**To WIN A FREE SEAT on Marco's Award Winning
LIVE ONE DAY WORKSHOP on the
Financial Freedom Guarantee worth $997
please scan and email your Book Purchase Receipt to:
ask@marcorobinson.com**

Printed in the USA
CPSIA information can be obtained
at www.ICGtesting.com
JSHW022342140824
68134JS00019B/1630